The Oceana Library on
The United Nations

This book is published by OCEANA PUBLICATIONS, INC.
in close co-operation with the United Nations

How to Plan and Conduct Model U.N. Meetings

A Handbook for Organizers

*Prepared by the United Nations
in co-operation with UNESCO*

NEW YORK

OCEANA PUBLICATIONS, INC.

1961

Copyright 1961 by Oceana Publications, Inc.

Library of Congress Catalogue Card Number: 61-15034

Printed in the U. S. A.

Contents

FOREWORD		VII
Chapter I	MODEL UNITED NATIONS SESSIONS	9
	Aims and Values	9
	Limitations and Difficulties	11
	Summary	12
Chapter II	PLANNING A MODEL SESSION	13
	Sponsorship and Co-operation	13
	Scope and Size of the Session	14
	The Organizing Committee	16
	Specimen Time-Tables	20
Chapter III	PREPARING THE AGENDA	23
	Common Mistakes	23
	Responsibility for the Agenda	24
	Arrangement and Circulation	25
	Criteria for Selection	26
	Number of Agenda Items	27
	Sources of Agenda Items	27
Chapter IV	SOURCES OF INFORMATION	29
	Major Types of Materials	29
	United Nations Materials	30
	Government Documents and Publications	36
	Other Sources of Information	37
Chapter V	THE MODEL SESSION DELEGATION	40
	The Task of the Delegation	40
	Selection of Delegates	40
	Advance Reading and Study	41
	Preparing Speeches and Position Papers	43
	Outline for Preparing a Position Paper	44
	Preparing Draft Resolutions	45
	At the Meeting	46
	Follow-up Activities	47
Chapter VI	CONDUCTING A MODEL SESSION	48
	The Model Session Programme	48
	The Physical Setting	48
	Seating Arrangements	49
	Plenary and Committee Meetings	50
	Plenary Meetings	50
	Committee Meetings	50
	The Role of the Presiding Officer	51
	Rules of Procedure	52
	Voting	53
	"Bloc" or Group Meetings	55

	Critiques and Reports	56
	Specimen Programmes	57
Chapter VII	MODEL SESSIONS OF UNITED NATIONS ORGANS	59
	The United Nations Family	60
	The General Assembly	62
	Functions and Powers	62
	Voting	63
	Sessions	63
	Organization	63
	Suggestions for Model General Assembly Sessions	64
	The Security Council	66
	Functions and Powers	67
	Voting	68
	Sessions	68
	Organization	68
	Suggestions for Model Security Council Sessions	69
	The Economic And Social Council (ECOSOC)	73
	Composition	73
	Functions and Powers	74
	Voting	75
	Sessions	75
	Organization	75
	Suggestions for Model ECOSOC Sessions	76
Chapter VIII	MODEL SESSIONS OF THE GENERAL CONFERENCE OF UNESCO	83
	Activities of UNESCO	84
	National Commissions	86
	Structure of UNESCO	86
	The General Conference	87
	Organizing a Model Session of UNESCO's General Conference	89
	Annotated Specimen Agenda Items	90
	Sources of Information about UNESCO	100
APPENDICES		
I	Speciment Letter of Invitation	102
II	Annotated Specimen Agenda Items	103
III	Specimen Resolutions	105
IV	Modified Rules of Procedure for a Model General Assembly	110
V	Modified Rules of Procedure for a Model Security Coucil	115
VI	A Selection of United Nations Documents and Publications	119
VII	United Nations Information Centres	124
VIII	Chart of the United Nations Family	127

Foreword

THIS HANDBOOK was prepared and written by the United Nations in cooperation with UNESCO. Its purpose is to provide practical suggestions on how to organize and conduct model sessions of United Nations bodies as a means of helping to extend and deepen public understanding of the aims and work of the United Nations and its related agencies.

The handbook was prepared in response to an increasing number of requests for information about model sessions which have come to the United Nations from many different countries. It is designed primarily for the use of teachers and students in secondary schools, and in colleges and universities. It is intended also to meet the needs of adult education groups and non-governmental organizations interested in sponsoring or participating in model United Nations meetings. Because of the complexity of subject matter and procedures concerned, it is unadvisible for model sessions of United Nations bodies to be attempted in elementary schools.

The aim of the handbook is simple: it attempts to answer the questions most frequently asked about model sessions. These include consideration of their educational values and limitations, the planning of sessions, the sources of information available, the preparation of "delegations," and the conduct of meetings.

To ensure that the suggestions put forward are practical, the handbook has drawn heavily on the advice and recorded experience of schools and organizations in various countries which have conducted model sessions of United Nations bodies. The helpful collaboration of the many persons and organizations concerned is much appreciated.

The Secretary-General wishes in particular to acknowledge the generous assistance of UNESCO in making this handbook possible.

OFFICE OF PUBLIC INFORMATION
UNITED NATIONS

CHAPTER I

Model United Nations Sessions

A MODEL SESSION of a United Nations body represents an effort to reproduce in essence the content and atmosphere of the public debates which do in fact take place in the various organs of the United Nations.

A model session can be limited to discussion of one topic in a single organ which has a small membership, such as the Security Council, the Trusteeship Council or the Economic and Social Council. A larger session might seek to portray typical plenary and committee meetings of a full or partial General Assembly or a General Conference of UNESCO, FAO or one of the other specialized agencies. In a model session, each participant represents a member country and tries to state, and obtain support for, the views actually held by that country on the subjects discussed.

Whatever its scope and size, the aim of a model session should be to deepen understanding of the purposes and work of the United Nations through intensive study and discussion of specific international problems which concern the world community.

As an educational experience, a model session is valuable if it results in informed debate on one or more world issues and a deeper appreciation by participants of the importance of international understanding and co-operation in the building of peace.

The decision to hold a model session should not be undertaken lightly. As an aid in considering the several factors involved, a summary of (1) the realistic educational aims and values, and (2) the chief limitations and difficulties of model sessions, is given below. This summary is based on advice and experience drawn from various countries.

Aims and Values

(a) Model sessions arouse keen interest, particularly among young people, in world problems and in the purposes and work of the United Nations. The enthusiasm of participants is perhaps the most marked characteristic of the model sessions. Most model

9

sessions are extra-curricular activities and usually do not carry academic credit. Yet, in preparation for a model session, many students devote very considerable time and effort to study of the United Nations and of the specific issues to be discussed.

A further indication of student interest is that, once begun, model sessions continue to be held in a particular school or region, year after year. The number of model sessions is increasing, not only in North America, but also in various countries in Europe, the Middle East, Asia, the South Pacific and Africa. Model sessions are also being used as a classroom teaching device in some secondary schools, and in a few colleges and universities.

(b) Well-run model sessions provide the educational values of debating. These include study and analysis of a serious subject, the preparation and defense of a reasoned position, and the development of skill in public speaking.

(c) Model sessions afford opportunities for practical exercises in education for international understanding. It is essential for a serious "delegate" at a model United Nations session to study and present the position actually held by the country he represents on a given issue, to find out the views held by other countries, and to try to win majority support for his position or achieve a workable compromise. In this process, participants should begin to appreciate the wide range of national interests and views which must be reckoned with in international life and thus gain a more balanced world outlook.

(d) Well-run model sessions can enrich the whole school and the community, as well as the participants. Often parents, teachers and the general public are invited to attend the sessions and find the experience both interesting and instructive.

(e) In some situations, model sessions attract the active participation and sponsorship of adult community organizations. For example, some of the large interscholastic model sessions, particularly in Canada and the United States, are organized and financed by organizations such as Rotary Clubs and United Nations Associations, working in partnership with the teachers and students of the participating secondary schools. The mature guidance and considerable resources thus brought to bear have yielded excellent results. These include the purchase of adequate study materials which become the property of the school of libraries and sustained study of these materials by the adult counsellors as well as by the students. As an added feature notable guest speakers are usually invited and typically provide further depth and distinction to the proceedings.

(f) Perhaps most useful in terms of education, model sessions can help students and others to understand more realistically the role of public debate in the practical operations of United Nations organs. It is not for nothing that such a lot of talk takes place in the world forums provided by the United Nations and its related agencies. For it is largely by means of these public debates that the national policies on world issues of the sovereign Member States are enunciated, the power of world opinion is invoked, and the mandates and authority for action by the United Nations organs are given.

Limitations and Difficulties

(a) It is not easy to hold a meaningful model session of a United Nations body. It requires accurate knowledge of the responsibilites and procedures of United Nations organs, careful selection and study of the subjects to be discussed, and serious individual and group effort to debate the issues effectively.

(b) A well-run model session involves the availability and use of considerable resources. These include skilled leadership, adequate study materials, sufficient time for preparation, and much hard work. Also, many of the basic documents and publications of the United Nations are issued only in the official or working languages of the United Nations body concerned. This fact presents a major difficulty in some countries. In educational institutions in which extra-curricular activities are not commonly held and encouraged, it may be difficult to find the necessary time.

(c) Experience shows that it is usually unwise for students to attempt to conduct model United Nations sessions unless the sustained guidance of mature and well-informed teachers and other knowledgeable adults can be secured. Qualified observers find, for example, that model sessions held by students in colleges and universities as largely self-directed extra-curricular activities are often inferior in preparation, content and presentation to adequately guided sessions held at the secondary school level.

(d) From an educational point of view, a poorly done model session is worse than useless. It can be positively misleading both to participants and to any observers so unfortunate as to be pres-

ent. The selection of unrealistic topics, lack of adequate preparation, indecorous behavior and the expression of uninformed views
can do positive disservice to the cause of the United Nations. It
cannot be emphasized too strongly that a model United Nations
session is not an appropriate channel for the conduct of fun and
games. The business of the United Nations is of the utmost seri-
ousness. Model sessions of its organs should not be held—ever—
in any other spirit.

(e) By their very nature, many important aspects of United
Nations work elude adequate portrayal through model sessions.
For example, in the political field, the delicate processes involved
in the negotiation, mediation and conciliation of many international questions cannot be pictured fully in public debate. In the
cultural field, model sessions cannot do much to assist understanding of UNESCO's important work in helping to acquaint a
wider public with the treasures of art and literature. This aspect
of UNESCO's work is done by means of calling attention to good
but inexpensive art reproductions and by promoting publications
of inexpensive editions of important literary works. Works of art
must be seen and literature read to be understood. In the field of
economic and social development, it seems likely that a clearer
view of the varied technical assistance activities of the United
Nations and its related agencies can be gained through the use of
films and filmstrips, or through the first-hand reports of experts,
rather than through model sessions. The point is that, for maximum effectiveness, model sessions should be used with discrimination, and in concert with other aids to learning.

Summary

The conclusion emerges that model sessions, if they are well-
run, have definite merits and usefulness. The available evidence
indicates that they can and do help to interest both young people
and adults in the work of the United Nations. In particular, they
provide a challenging opportunity to study and discuss important
world issues, to review national and world opinion on these issues, and to gain insight into the role and procedures of public
debate in United Nations bodies. Used with care, model sessions
provide yet another means to enrich the study of the United Nations and to further the process of education for international
understanding.

CHAPTER II

Planning A Model Session

IN ACTUAL PRACTICE, meetings of the United Nations and its related agencies are based on months of careful preparation by the Member Governments and the permanent Secretariats of the bodies concerned.

The process involves the construction and circulation of a provisional agenda and of basic studies and reports, most of which are prepared by the Secretariat. It then requires study of these documents by the member states, the proposal of additional items, and the preparation of position papers, speeches and draft resolutions.

Although the planning and preparation of a model session will obviously be much simpler, it must be done with care and precision for an effective session to result.

The basic steps which should be taken to organize a good model session are much the same for any United Nations body. These basic steps are outlined below using most often the United Nations General Assembly to illustrate content and procedure. Special features concerned in the meetings of the Security Council and the Economic and Social Council, are discussed in Chapter VII of this handbook. The General Conference of UNESCO is discussed in Chapter VIII.

To indicate the essential elements clearly, suggestions are given chiefly in terms of a model session which is to be held within a single secondary school, college or university, or adult group.

A larger meeting which involves the participation of many schools or groups contains the same basic elements. In addition, provision must be made to take care of further matters, essentially of a practical nature, such as considerable correspondence by mail with participants, food, housing, and possibly also social entertainment.

Sponsorship and Co-operation

A model session is necessarily a group enterprise. Hence, the first step is to explore the local school or community to see if a group can be interested. For student sessions, it is important also to enlist the co-operation of school authorities and relevant teachers (e.g., social studies, history, political science) to obtain expert programme assistance and to ensure the use of essential facilities, such as meeting-rooms and library services.

It would also be helpful to visit or write to the nearest United Nations Information Centre, to ask for advice on the content of the programme and to find out to what extent study material on topics of special interest can be made available. This is especially important in places where the language or languages used are not among the working languages of the United Nations bodies. A list of the United Nations Information Centres, with their addresses, is given in Appendix VII of this handbook.

If a well-informed teacher can be interested, the simplest procedure would be to hold a small session as a classroom exercise. In practice, however, most model sessions are extra-curricular activities, held under the sponsorship of one or more interested school or community organizations.

Model sessions in various countries have been sponsored by international relations clubs and institutes, local United Nations Associations, United Nations Student Associations, student unions, debating clubs, current events study circles, and community service organizations, particularly Rotary Clubs.

Joint sponsorship of model sessions is quite common in some countries. In the United States and Canada, for example, several large model sessions for secondary-school students are held yearly as projects sponsored by local Rotary Clubs, working jointly with teachers in the participating schools, and often also with other community organizations. At the same time, some of the large inter-university model sessions in these countries are sponsored entirely by *ad hoc* student-faculty "Model Session Committees", year after year.

In situations where well-established school or community organizations are not present, the formation of an *ad hoc* committee may be the only solution. However, where feasible, it is usually better to obtain the practical help and support of one or more sponsoring organizations.

Scope and Size of the Session

The first duty of the "sponsors" is to decide what type of model session is to be held and who shall be invited to participate. It is best to start simply and grow gradually. Hence, for a first venture, it is advisable to portray one organ only, preferably one with a small membership, such as the Security Council (11 countries) or the Economic and Social Council (18 countries). The agenda should be limited to one topic, although special features might be introduced as circumstances warrant. Such a feature might be the ceremony of seating newly-admitted member countries in the General Assembly; or it might be a well-prepared speech summarizing the findings of a basic study, such as the most recent *Report of the World Social Situation* or one of the yearly world or regional economic surveys, at a model meeting of the Economic and Social Council. In such first ventures participants should be drawn entirely from within one school, college or university, or adult education group, although the whole school or community might be invited to attend the session as observers.

As experience is gained, it may become feasible to portray a larger body such as a full or partial General Assembly of the United Nations or General Conference of UNESCO, with participants drawn from several or many schools. It should be noted that as the membership of the United Nations bodies increases, it becomes correspondingly necessary for model sessions to limit sharply the number of agenda items which can be considered and the time which can be allowed each "delegate" in the debate.

Increased numbers also multiply the practical difficulties involved in inter-school meetings, such as food and housing, without necessarily adding much to the substance of the debates. Although it is still too early for much recorded experience to be available on this point, it seems likely that future model sessions will find it advisable to ensure representation of each of the major geographical areas and of the various political, social and economic groupings rather than attempt to muster the full membership of the largest United Nations bodies. This, of course, is not an easy thing to do, since the actual alignments of member states in the United Nations bodies are for the most part quite fluid and vary considerably depending on the nature of the issue in hand. The alternative would be to hold the major discussion of most of the agenda items in two or three concurrently-scheduled committee meetings rather than in plenary sessions. This in fact is done in the actual sessions of the United Nations bodies.

It cannot be emphasized too strongly that large meetings should not be attempted unless skilled, mature leadership can be secured and the necessary resources, including adequate study materials, can be provided. Bigger does not necessarily mean better — indeed, rather the opposite tends to be the case in many model sessions.

The Organizing Committee

A carefully selected Organizing Committee should then be appointed (or elected) by the "sponsors." The task of this over-all committee, together with any sub-committees it may set up, is to plan, organize and guide the model session.

The Organizing Committee sets the date and place of the session and sends out notices of the meeting to the participants. It appoints the Secretary General and the Model Assembly officers. It also draws up and circulates the agenda, which is then considered as approved and adopted without further action being taken, at the opening of the model meeting. It assigns the country each "delegation" is to "represent," and acts as a Credentials Committee in that it receives and records the names of the participants. It also requests the various "delegations" to prepare appropriate resolutions within a time-limit fixed to permit circulation to participants well in advance of the meeting. It decides on and circulates the "Rules of Procedure" to be used. It draws up the over-all programme and time-schedule of the session. It appoints a Study-Materials Sub-Committee to work on documentation; and it appoints such other sub-committees as the needs of the session require. For a large inter-school meeting, these will usually include a Hospitality Committee to take care of registration, housing and food arrangements; a Secretariat to handle all conference paper work, such as correspondence, duplication and circulation of resolutions, etc.; a Publicity Committee; and possibly a Social Committee.

To make efficient work possible, the Organizing Committee usually should not have more than seven to nine members. For a small meeting, to be held within one school, most of the Organizing Committees should be students, working together with one or two keen faculty members and, if feasible, also a knowledgeable librarian. This pattern also works well for a large inter-school meeting at the college or university level. However, teachers and adults from the sponsoring organizations should take full responsibility for the planning of large meetings held for secondary school participants.

It may be useful to discuss in more detail some practical aspects of the work of the Organizing Committee outlined above. However, these suggestions are intended only to serve as general guidelines and should be adapted to suit local needs.

DATE AND PLACE: At least six weeks should be allowed for adequate preparation of a small intra-mural session. From four to six months is needed to prepare for a large session with many schools or groups participating. The physical facilities available often set practical limits to the size and scope of meeting which can be accommodated. If the whole school or the public is to be invited, steps must be taken to ensure that the audience can see and hear. This usually means that speakers must use a microphone. In North America and in some countries in Europe, it is common practice for some of the large model sessions (for secondary-schools, as well as those for college or university students) to be held on college or university campuses during a vacation period to permit use of the facilities of the host school for food and housing. However, model sessions in Asia and in most other regions are usuallly held during the school term.

SELECTION OF OFFICERS: Because participants should have adequate preparation for the roles they are to play in the conference, it is generally best for the officers to be selected by the Organizing Committee in advance of the meeting. The Secretary-General should be an outstanding student and should be a member of the Organizing Committee. In the case of a large meeting, he should be drawn from the host school. He is in charge of the work of the Secretariat, both before and during the model session meeting. The President presides over the plenary sessions and must know thoroughly the rules of procedure which are to be used. For large meetings, chairmen and rapporteurs of two or three committees may be needed. It may be noted that in the case of some large secondary-school meetings, the practice is for adults from the sponsoring organizations to serve as Secretary-General and President to expedite the conduct of the session.

ASSIGNMENT OF COUNTRIES: Methods in use vary. In some cases, participants choose the countries they wish to represent, indicating three choices in priority order; the Organizing Committee then does its best to meet the wishes thus expressed. Another method is for the names of the participants or the names of their schools to be placed in one hat and the member countries in another; by a simple draw from each hat, a participant is matched with a country. A third method is for an individual participant or school delegation to "show cause" in a brief written or oral discussion why the country chosen should be assigned, with the countries most in demand going to the individual or school that puts up the best case. In general, also, the practice is to rotate country assignments from year to year.

OUTSIDE SPEAKERS AND ADVISORS: If time and circumstances permit, an effective and well-known speaker will add distinction and depth to the meeting and help to create interest in the session. The possibilities include a present or former delegate to the United Nations General Assembly, or to whichever body is being portrayed; a visiting official of the United Nations; or an outstanding university professor or other authority on the topic to be discussed at the model session. The nearest United Nations Information Centre usually knows well in advance of the expected arrival of officials on mission in their areas.

Ideally such a person should speak at the opening or closing plenary session. The time at which it would be feasible for him to come might be a factor in determining the schedule of the session. The invitation should be sent in writing to the speaker well in advance of the meeting and should include full details; that is, it should include exact time and place of the session, the expected size and character of the audience (whether students, adults or both), and the agenda and time-schedule of the session. However, it should be stressed that the decision about obtaining a speaker depends very much on the total time-span of the session and the practical possibility of getting an appropriate person.

It is important to provide time at the opening session for a brief word of greeting from the head official of the host institution or sponsoring agencies concerned, and for a brief speech or vote of thanks to be given at the close of the session to those whose efforts made the meeting possible.

Planners of model sessions have also found it very helpful, when feasible, to invite an expert on United Nations affairs, such as the Director of the nearest United Nations Information Centre or a former or present member of the Secretariat of the body portrayed, to assist in planning the meeting and to observe the full session in action as a technical advisor. Such an advisor can also be used for consultation by the session officials while the meeting is in progress. A thoughtful and constructive appraisal at the closing plenary session by the technical advisor, indicating to what extent the real issues at stake have been portrayed in the debate, together with whatever other comments or suggestions he considers useful, is an effective way to ensure that any important distortions of substance are corrected for the audience and the participants. Such a critique, if well done, adds considerably to the value of the model session as an educational experience.

An interesting development in Canada is the widespread use of adult "counselors" in the large model sessions held yearly in the various provinces for secondary-school students. To bring mature advice and knowledge to the model session, each delegation of students is assisted during the four months of preparation by one or two counselors. Counselors include college and university professors, secondary-school teachers, members of the Canadian Institute of International Affairs, local United Nations Associations and Rotary Clubs. Counselors also attend the usual two-day model sessions. They sit at the table assigned to the delegation, but do not enter into the discussion on the floor at any time. Their role is advisory to the delegation in all its activities. In essence, this system is an adaptation of the role played by the permanent staff of the mission that each member nation maintains at United Nations Headquarters.

FINANCE: Obviously, the scale and cost of the meeting should be planned according to the resources available. It should be emphasized that a very good small meeting does not need to cost anything, if adequate study materials can be obtained through local school, university or public libraries, supplemented by such additional documentation as the nearest United Nations Information Centre can supply. Otherwise, a modest amount may have to be spent for key study materials.

In a one-day meeting, a good deal of effort and money can be saved by suggesting that the participants bring box luncheons with them, with possibly milk or other beverages available for purchase or free distribution, as resources allow. Housing and meal arrangements for a longer meeting must be determined by the facilities which the host school or sponsoring agency can make available. In some situations, these expenses are met chiefly by a registration fee paid by participants or their sponsors. In other cases, home hospitality is offered, especially for secondary-school students attending an out-of-town meeting.

Scrutiny of the budgets of several large inter-school meetings held in North America indicates that the chief items of expenditure are for study materials, including packets of basic documentation sent in advance to participants; stationery and postage; travel expenses of keynote speakers; and social entertainment. It will be seen that most of these expenses can be reduced sharply, or avoided altogether, if the meeting is kept small in scale and planned carefully with economy in mind.

Specimen Time-Tables

As an aid to organizers, specimen time-tables are given below to indicate the specific steps taken in planning two actual Model General Assembly sessions held recently in Canada for secondary-school students. The first shows the planning schedule for a session held in one school; the second is for a large session with many schools in a province brought together for a two-day meeting held in a large city.

A One-School Model UN Assembly

(Participants in a recent session included 46 students with 8 teachers acting as advisors)

10 September —Choose President and Secretary-General. These students must be intelligent and alert.

15 September —Decide which countries will be represented. Decide which classes will represent those countries. Decide the topic to be debated. Write the resolutions.

16 September —Choose the delegations and set up the class committees.

1 October —First meeting of the delegates. Explain what the United Nations is and what it does. Indicate problems posed by the resolution.

—Find keynote speaker. Arrange with local United Nations Association branch to bring greetings.

15 October   —Second meeting of delegates. Answer questions and help those who are having difficulty finding information.

1 November   —Committee meetings to plan discussion.

8 November   —Second meeting of committees.

15 November   —Afternoon: Bring desks to auditorium, set up delegation name cards. Delegations which are ready to speak at the opening of the debate give their names to Secretary-General.

    —Evening: Prepare microphone for use of President and Secretary-General on stage, and another for delegates speaking from a raised platform or rostrum on floor.

A District Model UN Assembly

(Participants in a recent session incluuded 160 students from 82 schools. 125 teachers and 80 community counselors acted as advisors)

1 July   —First meeting of the General Committee to plan the session. All committee members are adults selected by the Rotary Club and other sponsoring organizations in April at the close of the previous session of the Assembly.

1-30 August   —Preparation and mimeographing of all forms: invitations to schools; registration, resolution and amendment forms.

1 September   —Send out invitations to be returned prior to 30 September.

30 September   —Agenda to be drawn up during September and finalized by 30 September. Mail out agenda to counselors and participants.

1-15 October   —Select and present orders for presentation of basic study materials. A kit of basic documentation is sent to each participant; additional items are provided to advisors such as *Everyman's United Nations*. Participants are also advised to consult the current edition of the *United Nations Yearbook* which should be available in most public libraries or at the nearest United Nations Information Centre.

1 December   —Throughout this period, mail out letter to par-
1 February   ticipants and advisors as it is received.
15 March   —Final forms to be mailed to all participants.
                These include text of draft resolutions, creden-
                tial forms for participants and Counselors,
                travel instructions, and final copy of the pro-
                gramme.
26-27 April   —Holding of the Model Session Meeting.

CHAPTER III

Preparing the Agenda

THE NEED FOR exercising care and good judgment in preparing the model session agenda cannot be over-emphasized. A well planned agenda, circulated at the same time as the notice of the meeting, can do much to ensure adequate preparation by the participants and the smooth conduct of the session. On the other hand, a poorly drawn agenda constitutes a major handicap from which the session may not be able to recover.

Common Mistakes

The most common tendency is to overcrowd the agenda with far too many complex topics. The result is that there is not sufficient time either for participants to master the issues concerned in their advance study or for a meaningful discussion to be held at the session itself.

A second hazardous procedure, followed by many model sessions, lies in inviting participants to suggest items for the agenda and allowing their inclusion up to and even during the session itself. Even with a time-limit, this procedure involves circularizing participants several times in advance of the session. It thus requires time and secretariat facilities which few model sessions can or should spare for this purpose. In its most exaggerated form, it permits the proposal of "surprise" items at the session, on which most participants can have no preparation whatsoever. The only possible result is a time-consuming and fruitless "debate."

A third mistaken practice is that of including on the agenda "hypothetical" questions, with which the United Nations body being portrayed at the session has never dealt. Thus the "position" of the various countries can only imagined by the participants. In actual fact, a basic rule of the professional diplomat is that he simply will not discuss a "hypothetical" question which relates to his own or any other country. Model sessions would do well to follow this wise rule.

Responsibility for the Agenda

As indicated in Chapter II, it is suggested that the Organizing Committee assume full responsibility for determination of the model session agenda. Knowledge of United Nations affairs, and of the relevant documentation, are needed to draw up a well planned agenda; one or more members of the Organizing Committee should be selected with these requirements in mind. The Organizing Committee should also be fully aware of the capabilities of the participants and be able to gauge the extent and depth of preparation which can realistically be expected within the limits of the time and resources available. For student sessions, the advice of teachers in the participating schools should be sought on these matters.

As the central planning body, the Organizing Committee is in a strategic position to request counsel on the agenda from the nearest United Nations Information Centre, or information office of the specialized agency concerned. Although the busy schedule of United Nations officials makes it impossible for them to deal with requests for help from individual participants, they usually are able to give valuable advice to responsible organizers of model sessions on the selection of agenda topics and on the relevant documentation available.

The agenda as drawn up and circulated by the General Committee should be regarded as adopted, and requests for alterations or additions should not be admitted.

It should be noted that the basic procedures outlined above are provided for in the suggested "Model Session Rules of Procedure" given in this handbook. These will be found in Appendix IV, Rules 1 and 2. Although stated in terms of the General Assembly, these rules concerning the agenda should also be applied to model sessions of other bodies of the United Nations and its related agencies.

It should be stressed that the intricate procedure actually followed by the United Nations and most of its related agencies in drawing up the agenda of meetings should not be attempted by model sessions. First, it is impossible for a model session to simulate even approximately the skills and time of the Secretariats of the international organizations, the intermediate actions of the various United Nations bodies which often are involved, or the complex considerations weighed by governments in reaching a decision to request the inclusion of an agenda item. Secondly, the agenda of the United Nations bodies are planned for sessions much more extensive in time and facilities than those available to even the largest model session. For example, the agenda adopted by the 15th (1960) regular session of the United Nations General Assembly comprised 88 items. It included 73 items proposed by the Secretary-General in the provisional agenda issued on 22 July 1960, a supplementary list of 12 items proposed by member states and issued on 24 August 1960, and two items of "an urgent and important character" submitted by a member government for inclusion on 6 and 17 September before the session opened on 20 September 1960. The provisional agenda of the 11th (1960) regular biennial General Conference of UNESCO, drawn up by the UNESCO Executive Board included 22 items, with many sub-items. Since the largest model session can handle at most only four or five items, it is important that the careful selection involved should be done solely by the General Committee.

Enthusiasts of "democratic" agenda-making procedures may be comforted to remember that it is in actuality not easy, for a variety of reasons, to succeed in getting an item incluuded on the agenda of a United Nations body. Students of precedent may be relieved to realize that the procedure here suggested for empowering the General Committee to determine the agenda is in fact practiced by one of the oldest of the specialized agencies. The Governing Body of the International Labour Organization (ILO) has for many years exercised the unique power of fixing *definitively* the agenda of the annual ILO Conference.

Arrangement and Circulation

A list of the questions to be included in the agenda should be sent to the participants at the same time as the notice of the meeting.

Some organizers find it useful to include a brief explanatory note on each agenda item, outlining the background of the question briefly and the major issues concerned. This practice is usually helpful to participants in suggesting fruitful lines for study and for the preparation of draft resolutions. If a school or community audience is invited to attend the session, these notes are usually also included in a mimeographed or printed programme to assist the audience to follow the debate.

For a meeting which includes committees or commissions, as well as plenary sessions, the General Committee should also allocate the agenda items among the bodies concerned. The reader will find specimen agenda items in Appendix II.

Criteria for Selection

Topics selected for the agenda should be: (1) questions of major importance discussed at a recent session of the United Nations General Assembly, or whichever body is being portrayed by the model session; (2) questions on which adequate official documentation is published and readily available; and (3) questions of wide interest and of sufficiently general character as not to require the specialized knowledge of experts for presentation and comprehension.

It may be noted that a list of suggested agenda items for model sessions of the United Nations General Assembly, drawn up on the basis of these criteria, is issued in January of each year by the United Nations Office of Public Information and is available free on request from the United Nations Information Centres. The list is selected from the topics actually discussed at the most recent session of the General Assembly, and includes bibliographical references.

In this connection, it is interesting to note that the 11th (1960) regular session of UNESCO's General Conference for the first time included in its agenda discussion in plenary session of a topic deliberately chosen as "a question of general interest." The theme selected for 1960 was "The problem of international relations and exchanges in education, science and culture." This topic, carefully delimited to suit the time and major interests of the participants, at once suggests itself as a fruitful agenda item for a model session of a UNESCO General Conference. For example, a model session held in a teacher-training institution might concern itself exclusively with the question of international relations and exchanges in the field of education, while a session in a technical institute might focus its discussion on the field of science.

Number of Agenda Items

Three main factors should be taken into account in determining the number of agenda items: (1) the time available at the model session; (2) the time and resources available for preparation; and (3) the number of participants.

For a first effort, it is suggested that only one topic be discussed in a single plenary session of a United Nations body with a small membership, such as the 11-member Security Council.

As organizers and participants gain experience, it may become feasible to attempt a model session of a larger body, such as the Economic and Social Council with two or three of its Committees or Commissions, or a full or partial United Nations General Assembly or UNESCO General Conference.

Even then, it is suggested that the agenda be limited in a one-day session to not more than one major topic for full discussion in plenary session, and one further topic in each of not more than two Committees or Commissions.

A two or three-day model session, in which each "delegation" consists of three or four members, may wish to include a maximum of two topics for discussion in plenary sessions and two topics in each of three or four Committees or Commissions.

Throughout, organizers should be ever conscious of the need to guard against the danger of over-crowding the agenda. This peril besets large meetings especially, since generally there are time-consuming complications involved in the feeding and transport of sizable numbers of participants and also delays in moving from room to room when several committee meetings are scheduled. The excitement — and fatigue — attendant on the social entertainment which often accompanies large meetings should also be allowed for realistically. These are added reasons why it is suggested that only experienced organizers should attempt to hold large sessions.

Sources of Agenda Items

Organizers of model sessions should start the process of selecting topics for discussion by looking carefully through the actual agenda of the most recent session held by the United Nations body which is to be portrayed. This scrutiny will enable the organizers to see what issues actually are engaging the attention of the international body concerned and the stage which has been reached in their consideration.

The final agenda of the meetings of each of the United Nations bodies typically is issued in document form very shortly after the session opens and can usually be obtained on request from the nearest information office of the body concerned, as well as from its headquarters. These documents constitute the most swiftly-issued sources of information since they are intended primarily for the use of the delegates attending the session. However, they are not usually very meaningful, unless accompanied by relevant substantive material since they do not include any information except the titles of the questions and an indication of the allocation of the items to the committees or commissions concerned.

It is suggested, therefore, that organizers of model sessions would find it more useful instead to study the several sources of information which include discussion of the substance of the agenda items. These sources are reviewed in Chapter IV of this handbook.

CHAPTER IV

Sources of Information

To MAKE A realistic model session possible, organizers and participants must understand clearly the functions and work of the United Nations body concerned and study with particular care the specific agenda items to be discussed. For these purposes, a careful selection of study materials is essential but its extent need not be vast.

The selection of materials which should be made for a particular model session depends necessarily on which United Nations body is being portrayed and on the agenda topics. The extent to which materials are available in the area, through libraries and United Nations sales agents, and in needed languages, must also be taken into account. In many cases, funds for the purchase of materials are very limited. As these factors, singly and in combination, will vary considerably from one situation to another, it would be meaningless in a general handbook such as this to attempt to provide an ideal list.

Instead, the aim of this chapter is to point out the major types of materials issued and the purposes for which each is useful. Suggestions are also given on how to locate materials and how to approach the study of the various United Nations bodies.

For the convenience of readers, a selected list of United Nations documents and publications which provides full bibliographical details concerning the official materials cited in this chapter is given in Appendix VI.

Major Types of Materials

There are three major types of materials which organizers and participants in model sessions of United Nations bodies will find helpful. These are: (1) official documents and publications issued by the body concerned; (2) government documents and publications issued by the various countries "represented" at the model session to provide authentic background information concerning the country and its policies; and (3) other relevant materials issued in member states, including important studies, and major newspapers and periodicals.

Each of these categories of material is discussed below. However, main attention is devoted to official documents and publications issued by the United Nations and its related agencies since these constitute, in general, the key sources of information for model United Nations sessions.

United Nations Materials

There are four kinds of United Nations materials with which organizers of model sessions should be familiar. These are: (1) relevant pamphlets, leaflets and films issued by each agency to provide a quick overview of the functions and work of the body concerned; (2) basic general publications, including periodicals and reference books; (3) the rules of procedure and the official records, reports and resolutions of the body concerned; and (4) Secretariat studies and reports relevant to the agenda topics.

(1) PAMPHLETS, LEAFLETS AND FILMS: For groups which have not studied the United Nations systematically before, it would be useful to start by reading one or more of the general information leaflets and pamphlets issued by the United Nations and its related agencies. Selection depends upon the model session body and topics concerned.

A good first choice, because of its wide coverage, is *Basic Facts about the United Nations*. This pamphlet outlines the aims, structure and activities of the organs of the United Nations and its related agencies and shows how the various bodies are related to each other. It is issued in many language editions and frequently revised to provide current information. Other useful United Nations publications of this general type are *For Human Welfare*, a guide to the work of the Economic and Social Council; *Co-operation for Economic Progress*, which discusses the four regional Economic Commissions; and *Technical Assistance in Brief*, which discusses international technical aid through the United Nations. Copies of these items and lists of further such materials can be obtained from sales agents of United Nations publications in member states or from the nearest United Nations

Information Centre. They are also widely available in libraries in many countries.

The relevance of film materials will vary with the body and topics concerned. However, four recent films which would be directly useful to many model sessions have been produced by the United Nations on the United Nations Charter, the General Assembly, the Security Council and the Trusteeship Council. These are available in various language versions from official distributors of United Nations films in member states or from the nearest United Nations Information Centre.

(2) BASIC GENERAL PUBLICATIONS: Once past the stage of using the introductory materials noted above, four basic United Nations publications of major importance for model sessions are the *Charter of the United Nations, Everyman's United Nations*, the *United Nations Yearbook,* and the official monthly magazine, the *United Nations Review.*

The *Charter* is the ultimate authority on which the work of the United Nations and its related agencies rests. It sets out the purposes and principles of the United Nations, defines the conditions and procedures for membership, and establishes the structure and functions of the various organs. Relevant articles of the *Charter* are often cited in meetings of the United Nations bodies, not only in the speeches of delegates but also in the texts of resolutions, reports, and other documents. Hence, it is important for participants in model sessions to study it carefully and keep a copy on hand. It is widely available as a separate publication in many languages. It also appears as an appendix in *Everyman's United Nations* and the annual volumes of the *United Nations Yearbook.*

Everyman's United Nations (6th edition, 1959) is a compact reference book on the activities of the United Nations and its related agencies from 1945 through 1958. A new edition of this important book is issued about every three years. It is especially useful for looking up the historical background of particular topics, many of which are still actively under consideration by the various United Nations bodies. Individual topics can easily be located through the detailed index in the back of the book. For a small model session, held within a single school or group, one copy may suffice; organizers of larger sessions may find it useful to suggest that each participating school or group obtain a copy.

The *Yearbook of the United Nations,* issued annually since 1947, provides a full account of the activities of the United Nations and its related agencies during the year under review. Part I presents a summary of the discussions held and the action taken on each of the questions considered by the General Assembly and other United Nations organs, with extensive documentary references and the full texts of resolutions adopted. Part II surveys the activities of the other members of the United Nations family, including UNESCO.

Each yearly volume includes in an appendix the complete agenda of the sessions of the General Assembly, the Security Council, the Economic and Social Council, and the Trusteeship Council held during the year covered. It gives for each agenda item the plenary or committee meeting during which the subject was considered and the resolutions which resulted. Thus, organizers of model sessions will find it particularly useful to consult the most recent *United Nations Yearbook* as an excellent source of possible agenda topics, and for a concise review of the action which has actually been taken on each item as of the date given.

The monthly *United Nations Review* provides authoritative articles on the current activities of the United Nations and its related agencies, together with full coverage of the meetings of the General Assembly and other United Nations organs. Issued in separate English, French and Spanish editions and widely available in member states in libraries and from United Nations sales agents, it is an invaluable source of information for the use both of organizers and participants in model United Nations sessions.

A few additional comments about the *Review* may be helpful. The General Assembly meets in regular session beginning the third Tuesday in September. Each year, usually in its October issue, the *Review* carries the annotated provisional agenda and supplementary list of items for the current regular session of the General Assembly. This article, always entitled "Issues before the General Assembly" is swiftly reprinted as a separate pamphlet and is widely available through United Nations sales agents and from the United Nations Information Centres. The fact that it is annotated, issued regularly each year, and is easy to obtain makes it a particularly useful source for the selection of model session **agenda items.**

A further *Review* feature of special interest is the summary of the "general debate," which appears each year in the November issue, and which in 1960, for reasons of space, was continued in the December issue. It is in the "general debate," which takes place at the beginning of each regular session of the Assembly, that the heads of delegations state the views of their countries on urgent world problems of common concern to the United Nations and suggest courses of action for their solution. Thus, a review of the "general debate" provides a further guide to the selection of important agenda items. It also constitutes an invaluable source of information on the positions held by member states on major issues and can be used by model session participants preparing to "represent" their respective countries.

It should be noted that, throughout each Assembly session, the *Review* carries summaries of the debates held on the major agenda items; these summaries include the main points of draft resolutions considered and the main points of the resolutions adopted on these items. At the same time, a regular section of the *Review*, entitled "United Nations Digest" summarizes the proceedings and the decisions taken at each of the plenary sessions and committee meetings of the Assembly, with full documentary references. Finally, a survey of the main developments which have taken place during the Assembly appears in the *Review* immediately following the close of the session. This usually appears in the January issue.

Meetings of the other principal organ of the United Nations, such as the Security Council, are similarly covered as they occur.

It may be noted that, with an agenda limited to items of major importance, a very effective model session could be held using only the basic publications reviewed in this section as source material; that is, *Everyman's United Nations* for the historical background of the question, the annual volumes of the *United Nations Yearbook* to cover the period since the most recent edition of *Everyman's,* and the relevant issues of the monthly *United Nations Review* for current information.

Apart from the Rules of Procedure of the body concerned, the other official publications discussed below constitute primary sources of information which would considerably enrich and facilitate the model session, particularly in respect of the preparation of speeches and draft resolutions. However, if library resources in the area are sparse and the funds available for the purchase of materials are limited, participants in a model session find that the essential points needed for a meaningful and factually accurate debate are contained in summary form in the basic publications noted above.

(3) RULES OF PROCEDURE AND OFFICIAL RECORDS: Each principal organ of the United Nations and its related agencies determines its own rules of procedure to govern the conduct of its meetings. An example is *Rules of Procedure of the General Assembly*. These may be consulted in depository and other libraries or purchased from United Nations sales agents in member states. The reader will find full bibliographical details are given in Appendix VI.

Organizers of model sessions have generally found it helpful to modify the official rules somewhat, particularly in respect of the procedures to be followed in drawing up and adopting the agenda, the presentation of credentials, the election of officials, and the languages to be used. Typical modifications along these lines have been made in the specimen rules of procedure for model sessions of the General Assembly and the Security Council. These will be found in Appendixes IV and V of this handbook.

It should be noted that the rules of procedure of the various United Nations bodies have been established to meet the specific needs of the organs concerned and are amended from time to time as circumstances require.

For this reason, national parliamentary rules should not be used for the conduct of model sessions of United Nations bodies. Instead, a copy of the current official rules of procedure of the body to be portrayed at the session should be consulted by the organizers and the essence of the rules retained and used in modified form.

Official Records of the principal organs of the United Nations include the verbatim or summary records of the discussions of the plenary and main committee or commission meetings of the body concerned; reports and documents presented to the body or drawn up in the course of its discussions; and the resolutions adopted by the body during the session.

Verbatim records of the plenary meetings of the General Assembly and the Security Council are published in printed form, but only summary records are issued of the proceedings of the

Economic and Social Council, the Trusteeship Council, and the main committees of the General Assembly. Whether in verbatim or summary form, these records constitute the primary source of information on the positions taken by member states on the issues considered, the content and style of the speeches made, the draft resolutions proposed and the full course of the action taken, stage by stage.

Reports and documents presented to the United Nations organs are generally published as Annexes or Supplements to the *Official Records*. Among these reports, the *Annual Report of the Secretary-General* to the General Assembly and its separately-issued *Introduction* are of special importance. Together they provide not only a yearly survey of the major activities of the Organization but also a concise commentary on important current trends and events.

The Security Council, the Economic and Social Council, and the Trusteeship Council also present annual reports to the General Assembly. These are issued at the beginning of each regular session of the General Assembly, well in advance of the verbatim or summary records of the organ concerned. They provide a very useful guide for model sessions since they reflect the broad lines of the discussions held and actions taken. However, the full account is given only in the *Official Records*.

It should be noted that the *Resolutions* of the General Assembly and of the other organs mentioned above form part of the *Official Records* and are issued separately for each organ as Supplements to the *Official Records*.

Complete sets of the *Official Records* are kept in United Nations depository libraries in member states and are subscribed for for by some other large college, university and public libraries. Usually, the most recent records of the General Assembly and other principal organs of the United Nations can also be found in the United Nations Information Centres and may be consulted there.

The chief difficulty which model sessions experience in trying to use the most recent *Official Records* lies in the fact that, except for the *Reports,* they are usually not issued in printed form; they are therefore not available from United Nations sales agents until some six months or more after the close of the session of the body concerned.

However, limited numbers of the full set of documents which comprise the *Official Records* are issued during the session in provisional mimeographed form and can be consulted in depository libraries and in the United Nations Information Centres.

(4) SECRETARIAT STUDIES AND REPORTS: The substantive studies and reports prepared by the Secretariats of the United Nations and its related agencies on the agenda items provide essential facts and objective analyses of world problems for consideration and appropriate action by the decision-making organs.

These include, for example, periodic studies, such as the annual *World Economic Survey* and the biennial *Report on the World Social Situation* presented to the Economic and Social Council; the annual summaries and analyses of information, and the three-year special studies on economic, social and educational conditions presented to the General Assembly Committee on Information from Non-Self-Governing Territories. Ad hoc studies are also made on important current questions, at the request of the organ concerned. The report on the *Functions of a World Food Reserve* prepared by the Food and Agriculture Organization of the United Nations (FAO) is an example. This Report was prepared as a background paper for discussions which began in the Economic and Social Council in 1956 and led ultimately to the development of the United Nations World Food Plan adopted by the General Assembly at its 15th session in 1960.

A clear guide to the selection of relevant Secretariat studies and reports is provided by the current sales catalogues of publications issued by the United Nations and its related agencies (e.g., *United Nations Books in Print, 1960*), supplemented by the monthly *United Nations Documents Index*.

While summaries of some of the most important Secretariat studies and reports can be found in the official monthly magazine of the Organization concerned, obviously the educational value of the model session will be very considerably enhanced if participants locate and study carefully the full texts of the basic background documents relevant to the agenda items.

Government Documents and Publications

In addition to the United Nations materials described above, official documents and publications issued by the governments of the countries to be "represented" at a model United Nations session constitute a further helpful source of information. The scope, nature and availability of these materials vary greatly from one country to another. In general, however, there are two categories of government-issued materials which participants in model United Nations sessions will find useful.

First are the national materials which deal directly with United Nations affairs. It is often possible to obtain copies of important speeches, position papers and other materials relevant to specific agenda items discussed in current session of United Nations bodies, as well as popular leaflets and pamphlets on United Nations subjects, free on request to the nearest embassy, consulate or information office of the country concerned. These offices can also usually provide information concerning the availability and price of other relevant government publications, such as the extensive annual reports on national participation in United Nations affairs and other special studies issued in some countries.

Secondly, national government publications are a key source for obtaining basic facts concerning the country's geography, history and culture, as well as information about current trends, policies and problems in the political, social and economic fields. These factors are essential elements in understanding the national attitudes, aspirations and concerns of the country as these are expressed in the deliberations of the various United Nations bodies. Much useful general background material of this sort can be obtained free on request from the nearest embassy, consulate or information office of the country concerned. Important additional materials, such as the five or ten-year plans for economic development which constitute major guide-lines for many of the developing countries, are also widely found in university and other research libraries.

Care should be taken to ensure that materials used concerning the country are up-to-date, otherwise the data given can be very misleading.

Other Sources of Information

Considerable secondary source material on United Nations affairs and on the member countries can be found in many areas; these include articles and editorials in newspapers and magazines, pamphlets, reference books and monographs. However, it is important to seek expert advice in selecting the materials to be used since this wide range of sources varies very considerably in value and reliability. Depending on the nature of the topics concerned, much of it is also highly controversial.

While it is not possible within the compass of a brief handbook such as this to analyze these materials in detail, a few general guide-lines may be suggested to indicate various categories of materials and the purposes for which they are useful.

First, leading newspapers in many countries devote considerable attention to world affairs, including the United Nations. These newspapers typically provide full reports of the meetings of the United Nations bodies, particularly the General Assembly and Security Council; and they often include extensive summaries or the full texts of important speeches and reports. Thus, such newspapers generally constitute the swiftest and most widely accessible sources of information on current questions of importance and are invaluable for day-to-day study of United Nations affairs. They are also useful in providing a view of national attitudes and responsible public opinion on controversial issues in the various member countries.

Next, experts in United Nations affairs, including members of delegations, policy-making government officials, senior Secretariat specialists often contribute articles to serious journals on international affairs published in member states. Such articles are usually on timely topics and are often very useful in extending one's knowledge of a particular question or government policy and in gaining important new insights. Most of these journals are issued quarterly and are fairly expensive to buy. However, they are generally found in the larger research libraries, particularly in colleges and universities.

Standard reference books, such as encyclopedias, gazetteers and yearbooks, are widely found in libraries and are useful sources from which to obtain quick, up-to-date general information concerning member countries of the United Nations.

Finally, a very large number of reports and studies on the United Nations in general, and on specific aspects of its work and activities, have been issued in various languages in many countries throughout the world. Again, expert advice is needed in determining which among these varied materials are useful and reliable for the particular kind of information needed.

In summary, it should be emphasized that organizers and participants in model United Nations sessions will find that the most useful data for their purposes are, in general, the primary source materials, including particularly the official documents and publications issued by the United Nations and its related agencies.

CHAPTER V

The Model Session Delegation

The Task of the Delegate

EACH DELEGATE to a model United Nations session faces a challenging task. He must study carefully and be prepared to state, briefly and clearly, the position actually held by the country he "represents" on one or more major world issues. He must understand the views held by other countries on these issues, and be ready to defend and, sometimes, to modify his position in public debate.

He may have to draft, or amend, and must certainly vote on various resolutions. He may be expected to deliver a prepared speech at a plenary session or in a committee meeting. He may find it necessary to undertake informal negotiations with other delegations to rally support for a resolution, or make an impromptu statement explaining his vote.

As a voluntary participant in a group enterprise, each delegate should feel a deep sense of responsibility for the success of a model session. For no matter how skillfully the organizing committee has set the stage and drawn up the agenda, only the delegates can ensure that constructive and informed discussion of the issues concerned will take place and that the holding of the model session will result in a deeper understanding of how these issues are considered and acted upon through the processes and machinery of the United Nations.

Selection of Delegates

The size of the delegation and the assignment of countries should be determined by the central Organizing Committee, as indicated in Chapter II. Each participating group or school then selects its delegation.

For a small session, held within a single class or school, each delegation usually consists of not more than two or three people, who volunteer to serve or are elected by the class or other school groups concerned.

For large inter-scholastic meetings, more formal selection criteria and methods typically are used. In a regional session in Canada, for example, applications are invited, indicating that candidates should be students in the last two years of secondary school, with above-average scholastic records, willing to undertake intensive study and preparation, and with some experience or keen interest in public speaking and debating. Selection is then made by a joint committee made up of representatives of the sponsoring organizations, the secondary school headmaster, and one or two teachers. In colleges and universities, delegates are often elected by the campus international relations club or United Nations Association. In some cases, selection is made by a joint student-faculty committee, sometimes preceded by a written test on the United Nations devised and administered by the faculty.

In schools or communities which participate in model sessions year after year, an effort usually is made to include in each delegation some new members and some who have attended previous sessions. One of the senior members in experience is usually designated as head of the delegation.

For model sessions, as well as in actual fact, women are often selected as delegates to the various United Nations bodies.

Advance Reading and Study

Once the delegation is selected and has received its country assignment and the agenda from the central Organizing Committee, it should proceed to work out a systematic plan of individual and group study.

In this connection, every effort should be made to enlist the help of a knowledgeable and interested faculty member to work with the delegation in preparing for the meeting and to act as its expert adviser at the model session itself. If available, the delegation should also seek the aid of a skilled librarian in locating needed information with a minimum of waste motion. It is very helpful also if the key materials needed can be assembled and kept together in a particular place in the library stacks or reading room during this intensive period of preparation.

Each delegation should begin its study by looking at the coun-

try it is to represent, as a whole. What are the salient features of
its geography, its history, its people, its government, its economic
and social development? To what important regional or international organizations or other formal or informal groupings does
it belong? What are its major problems and pre-occupations in
international affairs? Throughout, the effort should be made to
come to know not only what positions on major questions the
country has taken, but why it has done so. To achieve best results
quickly, certain aspects of the study should be assigned to each
member of the delegation, with joint meetings to share the fruits
of everyone's labour.

A division among delegation members of the topics to be discussed will also facilitate preparation. Thus, each person can
develop fairly expert knowledge on one or more of the issues on
the agenda and can act as the delegation spokesman at the plenary sesions or committee meetings dealing with his particular
subjects.

An interesting feature used to help delegations with their ad-
vanced preparation is used by the model General Assembly held
each year in the Toronto School District of Ontario, Canada.
Representatives from Toronto's large consular corps and graduate
students from the University of Toronto, representing as many
countries as possible, are invited to meet with the student delegations. Sitting at tables marked by country, the model session
delegates ply these special advisors with questions about the
country and its policies, and thus gain invaluable background.

Then the real working sessions begin. They are held at one of
the colleges of the University of Toronto on four Saturday after-
noons throughout the autumn. With the delegates arranged
under the topic of agenda item, each group is briefed by faculty
members and other subject experts; questions and group discussions form a part of each briefing session. The delegates also read
and study independently.

In addition to preparation on the agenda topics, the delegation
as a whole should review carefully the purposes, structure and
major current activities of the United Nations body to be portrayed at the session; they should be very clear on the relations
of the body concerned to the United Nations family as a whole.
The whole delegation also should study carefully the rules of
procedure which will be used at the model session.

A few suggestions concerning reading and note-taking may be useful. Research in this field indicates that it is far more effective to focus your study on a limited number of carefully selected sources than to attempt to wade through vast masses of material.

It is also good study technique to read a speech, article or pamphlet quickly and all the way through the first time, without stopping to take notes. Thus, you can follow the content of what you are reading without distraction. Then, if you wish to take notes, you can do so quickly and in brief outline form since you will understand exactly which points really are important.

A note of reminder — some basic sources of useful study materials, with a brief guide to their use, are described in Chapter IV of this handbook.

Preparing Speeches and Position Papers

Preparing and delivering speeches in public debates are major activities in the life of a delegate to a United Nations body. The participant in a model session must also expect to engage in these activities.

In general, two main kinds of prepared speeches are made to United Nations bodies. One is the over-all statement of policy usually made by the head of the delegation, outlining the views held by his government on major matters of world concern. Such speeches are made each year by most delegations to the United Nations General Assembly during the "general debate," which is always held at the beginning of each regular session of the Assembly.

The second type of speech, which is made far more frequently, is limited to a specific topic on the agenda. In actual practice it will be found that the formal debates on matters of substance before the various United Nations bodies typically consist of carefully prepared written statements during which the delegations outline the considered positions of their respective governments on the subject under review.

It is of major importance that participants in model sessions should recognize, as indeed the member governments have done, that the complex issues which are considered by the international organizations require thorough advance study and preparation for useful discussion to take place.

The agenda prepared by the central Organizing Committee should indicate whether or not a "general debate" will be held and, if so, the amount of time to be allotted to each speaker. The usual time given is not more than five to ten minutes, depending on the number of speakers, and it is strictly enforced.

This speech should obviously be based on the most recent such speech actually made in the general debate by the country concerned, with its main points condensed to meet the time limits set by the model session. All members of the delegation may wish to collaborate in its preparation so as to secure an agreed text. The speech usually will be delivered at the model session by the head of the delegation.

Meanwhile, a position paper should be prepared on each agenda item. Each topic should be assigned to some one person on the delegation as his particular responsibility. A suggested outline for use in the preparation of a position paper is given below, adapted from a text prepared by students at the San Francisco State College (USA) :[1]

Outline for Preparing a Position Paper

A. Background of agenda item in the United Nations.
  1. The problem or issue involved.
    (a) Main elements of the problem.
    (b) General positions of importance on the issue, e.g., position of major powers, blocs, and other countries.
    (c) Action taken on the issue, e.g., UN resolutions adopted, Secretariat studies or surveys made, and referrals to other bodies, such as World Court.
B. Your country's position on the issue.
    (a) Check UN sources, including speeches, votes on resolutions adopted, and draft resolutions proposed to determine its past position.
    (b) Study comments on the issue in national press, parliament, periodical articles, speeches of leading government officials and subject experts.
    (c) List the objectives sought and identify expected sources of support and oppositon. Outline strategy

---

1. *Model United Nations Handbook*, by B. V. Wehrly and D. G. Sherlock. San Francisco, San Francisco State College, 1960. 102 p. (Photo-offset).

for introducing resolution and securing sponsors
and insuring supporters.

C. Justification of the position and summary.

    (a) Main reasons supporting your country's point of
view.

    (b) Strongest reasons in favour of opposing positions
and your points in rebuttal.

    (c) Presentation of your draft resolution.

The position paper should be written down in outline form
and reviewed with the other members of the delegation and with
the faculty adviser to obtain their suggestions. This procedure
will also provide useful practice in making the presentation before a critical but friendly audience.

At the model session itself, it will add much to the interest and
spontaneity of the proceedings if prepared speeches are not read
verbatim. Instead, the main points to be covered should be noted
in outline form and referred to only as often as is necessary for
the speaker to maintain the orderly sequence of a reasoned and
well-prepared position.

Preparing Draft Resolutions

Most decisions of United Nations bodies are expressed in the
form of resolutions. Resolutions typically are submitted in draft
form under the sponsorship of one or sometimes several delegations, and are usually discussed first in committee or commission
meetings, where the draft text may undergo several amendments
before approval. The resolution as approved by the committee
then goes to the plenary session of the organ concerned for final
consideration, which will result in its adoption or rejection.

It is important to have some resolutions prepared in advance,
to ensure an orderly start of the session. Certain delegations
should be asked to prepare draft resolutions and submit them to
the central Organizing Committee in time to permit mimeographing and distribution to all participants at least several days before
session starts. The nature of the topic and the presumed main
positions will determine the assignment of resolutions.

This procedure does not, of course, preclude the submission of
other resolutions by interested countries, both before and during
the session. However, even in a small meeting, experience indicates that it is wise to encourage delegations to submit resolutions

in advance since this enhances the possibility of securing well-prepared resolutions and reduces the burden of Secretariat work in mimeographing and distribution to be done during the session.

Resolutions generally consist of two parts: a preamble and an operative section.

The preamble is designed to explain the purpose of the resolution and to state the main reasons in support of the operative sections which follow. The preamble often refers to earlier United Nations resolutions or other actions taken on the matter. Reference is also often made to some appropriate article in the United Nations Charter. Similarly, resolutions presented or addressed to a specialized agency may refer to the constitution of that agency.

The operative sections of a resolution take the form of recommendations for action, or a statement of favourable or unfavourable opinion concerning an existing situation. The resolution may request action by member states, or by the Secretariat of the organ concerned, or by other bodies of the United Nations family.

Resolutions should be carefully thought out and, in general, follow actual United Nations practice in substance, although often in simplified form. Examples of United Nations resolutions are given in Appendix III of this handbook. However, resolutions submitted to and adopted by model sessions will usually be shorter and expressed in more every-day language.

At the Meeting

The head of the delegation, with his colleagues, should report immediately on arrival at the model session to the place designated by the Organizing Committee. Here the delegation will receive its kit of documentation for the session including its identification tags (i.e. "credentials") and, if appropriate, instructions concerning meals, housing and the like.

In a large model session, meetings of the delegation members should be planned to ensure co-ordination of the positions taken by them at the various committee meetings and plenary sessions.

Most model sessions must be run on a very close time schedule. The task of the Organizing Committee will therefore be much facilitated if each delegation will be on time for all scheduled events, including meals and any social activities, as well as all plenary and committee meetings. It should also be taken for granted that delegates will conduct themselves with decorum at all times.

Follow-up Activities

The excellent work which is often done by model session organizers and delegates alike should be used as widely as possible. Delegations should keep records of their prepared speeches and position papers. These might be turned in to the central Organizing Committee for use as background data for future meetings. Special documentation purchased or obtained free from embassies, Permanent Missions or other sources should usually be given to the school library to enrich its United Nations collection. It is also often useful for each delegation to write a report on the model session, giving special attention to suggesting ways in which future model sessions might be improved.

CHAPTER VI

Conducting A Model Session

THE RESPONSIBILITY for conducting the model session efficiently rests on the Organizing Committee, working closely with the conference officials. (The President and chairmen of the various committees) , and the Secretariat. Again it should be stressed that careful advance planning is essential, and also that the larger the session, the harder it will be to run it well.

The Model Session Programme

A tentative schedule, giving dates and indicating the content and time alloted to plenary sessions, committee and other meetings, and meals and social events, should be worked out by the Organizing Committee and sent to participants as soon as possible This provisional programme constitutes a draft work-plan for the model session and will be found very helpful to participants and organizers alike in preparing for the session. This procedure also makes it possible for changes in the programme to be suggested and incorporated in advance of the meeting.

As soon as the names of outside speakers and other details are confirmed, a final programme should be drawn up and mimeographed or printed in sufficient copies to permit distribution to individual participants and to the audience at the start of the session. It may be useful to note that quite often advertising space in the programme can be sold to meet the costs of printing.

Once the programme is established, it is very important to follow the time schedule given with as few changes as possible. Otherwise, confusion will almost certainly result.

Specimen programmes for meetings of three different lengths are given at the end of this chapter.

The Physical Setting

The place in which the model session is held can enhance or

impede the effectiveness of the meeting. The setting need not be elaborate but it should be accessible, adequate in light and ventilation, and large enough to seat the participants and audience comfortably. Overcrowding of any kind should be carefully avoided. This can only be ensured by planning the size of the meeting realistically to fit well within the limits of the available facilities.

A small committee should be placed in charge of room arrangements, including decoration. Tables or desks will be needed for delegations and presiding officers, plainly marked with signs indicating the names of the member countries and the titles of the chief conference officers. Such signs can easily be made using cardboard lettered legibly by hand to permit the signs to be read from both the back and front of the room. A microphone for the use of speakers usually is needed. Care should be taken to ensure that it is in good working order before the meeting begins.

The United Nations flag and those of member states make particularly effective and appropriate decorations. Sets of flags can be rented from commercial companies in some places, or they can be borrowed in some areas from the nearest United Nations Information Centre or local branch of the United Nations Association. Exhibits using a selection of the photographic display sets issued by the United Nations and its related agencies, or other photographs depicting the work of the United Nations in various parts of the world, together with selected posters and maps can provide further interest and information to the session, and also add considerably to the attractiveness of meeting rooms and corridors.

Seating Arrangements

It may be of interest to note that countries are seated in the actual sessions of the General Assembly in English alphabetical order, starting in the front row, left to right, with the country whose name is pulled out of a box at random at the first meeting of the session concerned. If desired, the seating arrangement followed at the most recent session of the General Assembly can be obtained free on request from the nearest Unitd Nations Information Centre.

If feasible, it is desirable to seat delegates during small committee and Council sessions in a horse-shoe or round-table arrangement to facilitate face-to-face discussion.

Plenary and Committee Meetings

Model sessions of the General Assembly usually follow actual United Nations practice in organizing their work into plenary meetings of the whole Assembly, and committee meetings in which each country is represented by one delegate. This pattern is also generally followed in the regular sessions of the main deliberative organs of other members of the United Nations family, such as the General Conference of UNESCO.

Items on the agenda, as a rule, are allocated to the main committees for their consideration and recommendation. However, the Assembly itself, acting directly in plenary meeting, deals with items not referred to a main committee.

Plenary Meetings

Plenary meetings are usually held at the opening and closing of a model session. Because of the exigencies of time, each meeting typically includes several events, as indicated in the specimen programmes given at the end of this chapter. Most model sessions have found it particularly effective to include a general debate at its opening plenary. In view of the increasing membership of the United Nations organizations, it is essential to limit strictly the number of speakers, usually to not more than six or eight; and each speaker should be allotted three to five minutes for his remarks. The usual method is to select countries which represent the main geographical regions and political groupings, rotating the particular countries selected each year. Delegates from the countries selected are asked to prepare their speeches in advance.

Other effective features for plenary meetings include the admission of new members (with one selected as spokesman) and an address by a distinguished outside speaker.

As a practical matter, it should also be borne in mind that plenary meetings afford the most convenient and in large-scale sessions, the only sure means of reaching participants with announcements of changes in schedule and the like.

Committee Meetings

Except in the Security Council, most of the substantive questions on the agenda of the various United Nations bodies are referred to established or *ad hoc* committees. Each committee deals with a different aspect of the body's work.

Each committee discusses in detail the one or more questions assigned to it and adopts a draft resolution on each. The rapporteur of the committee then draws up a report summarizing the main points of the discussion on each item and presents this report, together with the draft resolutions adopted by the committee, to the plenary session. There the reports of the committees are approved and the resolutions adopted as drafted by the committee, usually without much change.

It is important to note that in actual United Nations practice the main speeches on questions referred to committees are made in committee and not in plenary meetings. Howver, protracted debate sometimes does take place in plenary sessions in cases where the vote in the committee has been close or where several delegations wish to emphasize their special positions on an important matter. In model sessions, the pressure of time usually makes it necessary to limit debate to not more than two speakers in favour and two opposed, with three to five minutes allowed to each speaker.

The Role of the Presiding Officer

Skillfull presiding officers (i.e., the President and the committee chairmen) are of crucial importance to the conduct of an effective model session. Except in very small sessions, students should usually not be called upon to act in this very demanding capacity, at least until after they have had the opportunity to participate in previous model sessions as delegates. Even then, they should be known to have mature and well-balanced personalities and considerable mental agility. It is worth stating again that the selection of effective presiding officers should be regarded as a matter of major concern by the Organizing Committee.

The first task of a presiding officer is to regulate the debate. It usually aids lively discussion if initial speeches are kept short (two or three minutes) both to ensure widespread active participation within the group and also to enable the main positions on an issue to be placed before the group quickly.

The presiding officer should also keep the debate focussed on the matter under discussion and guide it into constructive channels. He should discourage persistent irrelevancies with tact and good humor. This can usually be done by saying pleasantly to the participant concerned, "I think I understand your point, but could you help us by explaining how it bears on the issue now under discussion?" If he cannot, he is usually willing to drop the matter. Sometimes, also, such points really *are* important to later stages of the discussion and the chairman should request that the matter be deferred until the appropriate time has been reached.

It is, of course, essential that the chairman maintain strict impartiality and not engage in controversy on the matters of substance under discussion.

It is also the duty of the chairman to ensure that the discussion progresses steadily to an orderly conclusion. At the right time, it is usually helpful to summarize the main points of the discussion briefly, indicating those on which agreement has been reached, and then suggesting that the points of disagreement which remain be considered each in turn.

If the delegates are well prepared, this process will usually help to bring about some measure of agreement, often simply by the re-drafting of a phrase or paragraph in a resolution or the proposal of an acceptable amendment.

If it proves to be impossible to reach agreement, the chairman should ensure that the group is given full opportunity to understand the various opposing positions and the reasons why each is being held.

However, participants should never lose sight of the fact that in model sessions, as in the United Nations itself, the main object sought is reduction of the areas of tension and disagreement and the achievement of a workable synthesis of conflicting views. Indeed, a major result of the model session for each participant should be enlarged understanding of views other than his own and increased recognition of the need to accept and understand compromises as a major fact of international life.

Rules of Procedure

It is very important that the limited time of the model session not be wasted in arid debates on procedure. Firmness and skill on the part of the presiding officers are crucial in this regard. Indeed, the Organizing Committee should specifically request the presiding officers to dispose of procedural points as quickly as possible in order that the full attention of the session can be focussed on the substance of the debate.

In addition, two further practical steps are usually helpful in dealing with this matter. The first is to ensure that copies of the rules of procedure which will be used at the session are distributed to the individual participants and to their faculty advisers well in advance. It is wise to accompany the rules with a note requesting that they should be studied carefully since at the meeting itself a good working knowledge of the rules will be taken for granted and points of procedure will be disposed of very quickly.

A second helpful procedure is to have the presiding officer make a brief statement at the opening plenary meeting and possibly also at the start of the committee meetings; this should cover such practical matters as the time limits to be allowed in debates. Time should be allowed to answer any questions which participants may wish to raise.

Voting

Each deliberative body within the United Nations family has its own voting arrangements, which are set forth in detail in the official rules of procedure of the body concerned. For the main organs of the United Nations, provisions concerning voting are also given in the Charter and, in the case of the specialized agencies, in their constitutions.

However, it may be useful here to outline the salient features of the voting procedures followed in the General Assembly, since for the most part, similar procedures obtain also in the General Conference of UNESCO and in the main deliberative bodies of most of the specialized agencies.

In the General Assembly, and typically throughout the United Nations system of organizations, with the exceptions noted below, each member country of the body concerned has one vote and every vote is equal.

The unique voting arrangements of the Security Council, including the "veto" are discussed in the next chapter. Quite different special features also characterize the voting procedures followed respectively in the International Labour Conference of the International Labour Organization (ILO) and the Governing Councils of the International Bank for Reconstruction and

Development (the World Bank), and the International Monetary Fund.

In plenary meetings of the General Assembly, decisions on important questions (e.g., admission of new members, budgetary matters) require a two-thirds majority of the members present and voting. Other questions are decided by a simple majority. Voting in committees and sub-committees is also by simple majority.

Although nowhere so stated in the Charter, by prevailing practice now embodied in the rules of procedure of the various United Nations organs, the phrase "members present and voting" means members casting a negative or affirmative vote. Abstentions from voting are considered as not voting.[1] The effect of this rule is that the majority required for adoption of a measure is calculated on the basis of the number of affirmative and negative votes. If this were not so, an abstention would in fact count as a negative vote.

Voting normally takes place by show of hands, but any delegate may request a roll-call. A vote by show of hands goes into the record simply as total numbers for, against and abstaining. Hence, a roll-call vote is sought if a detailed record of the vote by country is desired. This method of voting is very time-consuming and is usually resorted to only in connection with highly controversial or important questions.

The roll-call is taken in the English alphabetical order of the names of the member countries, beginning with the country whose name is drawn by presiding officer at random out of a box containing slips with the names of all member countries of the body concerned. The name of each member country is then called out by the secretary of the meeting and each delegation votes by replying orally "Yes," "No" or "Abstention" as its name is called. The result of the vote thus taken is placed in the record in the English alphabetical order of the member countries, with a summary showing the names of members for, against and abstaining.

As a general rule, model sessions of the General Assembly have found it best to request the presiding officers to limit the number of roll-call votes permitted both in plenary and committee meet-

---

1. For full discussion, see: *Reportory of Practice of United Nations Organs*, New York, United Nations, 1955, Vol. I, pp. 565-598; also *Supplement No. 1*, Vol. I (1958), pp. 194-203.

ings. In large-scale sessions, the usual practice is to allow a limited number of roll-call votes in committee meetings, and preclude their use altogether in plenary meetings.

A few further notes concerning voting rules and practices in the General Assembly may be useful, since parallel procedures are widely found in other bodies within the United Nations system of organizations. The first of these is that, by rule, all elections in the General Assembly are held by secret ballot, and there are no formal nominations. As a practical matter, this actual procedure can usually not be followed in model sessions.

What is far more important for model sessions to note is that, in practice, proposals representing decisions of the General Assembly frequently are considered as adopted without a formal vote being taken. Thus, for example, applicant States typically are admitted to the United Nations "by acclamation" once the Security Council has recommended their admission, rather than by actual vote of two-thirds majority of the members present and voting as specified in the Charter. Draft resolutions recommended by committees are usually declared by the President of the General Assembly in plenary meetings as adopted in the absence of objections.

It should also be noted that, both in plenary and committee meetings, procedural matters are most often decided as suggested by the presiding officer, with the tacit consent of the members. In brief, it is rare for rulings on procedure made by the presiding officer to be challenged in the various United Nations bodies. Model sessions would do well to ensure that their meetings also are conducted by skillful presiding officers and then follow United Nations practice in focussing their attention on the substance of the matter under consideration and not on the gossamer intricacies of procedure.

"Bloc" or Group Meetings

It has become customary in some model United Nations sessions, particularly of the General Asembly, to set aside specific time in the schedule for "bloc" or group meetings. These are also sometimes called "caucus meetings." The aim of these meetings is to provide time for the members of various designated groups to work out the details of the main positions they will take up on the agenda items and to secure the votes of group members on these items. This practice is definitely not recommended. Instead, it is suggested that the time of the model session could be used far more profitably by extending the time available for substantive discussion of the agenda items in committee and in plenary meetings, and eliminating altogether any form of "caucus meeting."

A brief word of further explanation may be useful. In actual practice, the process of informal consultation and negotiation on issues under consideration in the various United Nations bodies sometimes takes place in private meetings of groups of states, which are sometimes referred to as "blocs." No public records of these meetings are kept. Moreover, since such meetings are for the most part flexible and, in several cases overlapping in membership, as well as unofficial in character, even their group identities can only be approximated. However, the chief groupings are usually assumed to include the Latin-American countries, the British Commonwealth countries, the Afro-Asian countries, the Communist countries, the Arab League countries, and the Western European or North Atlantic Treaty Organization (NATO) countries.

In fact, it is clear from the positions held in debates and the votes taken in the General Assembly and other United Nations bodies that the degree of cohesion which exists within the various groups varies considerably in relation to the particular issue concerned. This fact, coupled with the absence of public records of the proceedings of such group meetings, would seem to make any effort on the part of model session to simulate "bloc" meetings distinctly unrewarding.

Critiques and Reports

At the end of the model session, it can be very helpful for a brief but thoughtful commentary on the proceedings to be made orally by a qualified person who has been in a position to observe the whole session. Depending on the practical circumstances, such a person might be a former delegate to an actual session of the United Nations body portrayed at the model session, the Director of the nearest United Nations Information Centre or other member of the Secretariat in the area, a knowledgeable university professor, or an official or member of the local United Nations Association.

Organizers of those model sessions which have been held year after year in some areas have usually found it useful to prepare a final report on the session, with suggestions for improving future sessions. In this way, the clues gained by experience can be recorded and transmitted, not only to succeeding members of the Organizing Committee, presiding officers and other conference officials, but also to all future participants and their faculty advisors. In the course of preparing this report, follow-up meetings of the organizing committee are sometimes held after the close of the session; or written statements are sometimes requested from the relevant committee members and conference officers for inclusion in the report. Usually such reports are mimeographed in limited quantities and are available free on request from the organizers while the stock lasts.

Specimen Programmes

As a practical aid to organizers of model sessions, specimen programmes adapted from several used in recent model General Assembly meetings are given below. The specific elements included in these programmes and the time allotted to each are indicated.

ONE-EVENING SECONDARY-SCHOOL SESSION

8:00 - 8:05 p.m.	Opening speech by the Assembly President
8:05 - 8:10	Words of welcome (school headmaster)
8:10 - 8:11	One minute of silent prayer or meditation
8:11 - 8:15	Greetings from local United Nations Association
8:15 - 8:30	Keynote speech (outside speaker)
8:30 - 9:30	Debate on the resolution
	(First speaker should outline the background of the question and present a draft resolution)
9:30 - 9:45	The vote (taken and announced)
9:45 - 9:55	Word of summary and thanks by Secretary-General
9:55 - 10:00	School song

One-Day District Secondary-School Session

9:00 - 9:25 a.m.	Registration
9:30 - 10:55	Plenary meeting of the Assembly
	Welcoming speech by President
	Admission of new members (one spokesman)
	General debate (six speakers)
11:00 - 12:15 p.m.	Committee Meetings
	Political Committee
	Economic Committee
	Social Committee
	Trusteeship Committee
12:30 - 1:30	Box lunch
1:45 - 2:45	Committee Meetings Resumed
3:00 - 4:30	Final plenary of the Assembly
	Report from each Committee, with vote on each Critique of the meeting
4:30 - 4:45	Closing speech (outside speaker)
4:45 - 4:55	Word of thanks by Secretary-General
5:00 - 6:00	Tea and social hour

CHAPTER VII

Model Sessions of
United Nations Organs

EACH ORGAN of the United Nations and its related agencies has
its own specific functions, powers, procedures, and methods of
work which must be taken into account in planning model sessions of the body concerned. It is also important to understand
the relationships which exist between the various organs and
agencies which comprise the United Nations system.

Thus, the purpose of this chapter is to provide brief background information on the United Nations family in general and
to provide more detailed information on the functions and operation of the organs of the United Nations which are most frequently presented in model sessions: The General Assembly, the Security Council, and the Economic and Social Council.

In similar fashion, Chapter VIII, which has been prepared by
the UNESCO Secretariat, will discuss the organization and work
of UNESCO and provides practical suggestions on how to plan
and conduct model sessions of the UNESCO General Conference.

It should be stressed that full information concerning the structure and work of the United Nations system of organizations is
available in the official publications described in Chapter IV,
particularly in the frequently revised pamphlet *Basic Facts about
the United Nations,* the useful reference book *Everyman's United
Nations* and the comprehensive annual *Yearbook of the United
Nations.*

However, the brief notes given below may provide a convenient
summary and also some general guide-lines which can be used,
with necessary adaptations, in organizing model sessions of other
United Nations bodies.

It should also be noted that the present handbook is intended
to be read and used as a whole. Thus matters of general relevance

to the planning and conduct of model sessions of United Nations bodies which have already been discussed in previous sections of the handbook are not dealt with again in the pages which follow, except where it has been considered useful to add further details. Instead, the reader is requested to consult the section concerned, using the Table of Contents given in the front of the book as a guide.

The United Nations Family

At the outset, a major concept should be made clear: The United Nations is not a single monolithic organization. It is instead a co-ordinated system composed of many associated international bodies and agencies which work closely with member governments and with each other to advance the aims expressed in the United Nations Charter: peace and economic and social development of all mankind. This partnership of international organizations has come to be known as the United Nations family.

The relationships between the various United Nations bodies can be seen in the chart entitled "The United Nations and its related agencies" (See Appendix VIII). It is useful to study this chart, especially since questions discussed in one body, such as the General Assembly, are often referred for appropriate action or further study to another body of the United Nations itself, such as the Disarmament Commission or the Trusteeship Council, or to one of the associated agencies, such as UNESCO, depending on the subject matter concerned.

It is important also to realize that the associated agencies which make up the United Nations family are separate, autonomous organizations although they are related to the United Nations by special agreements. Each has its own membership, its own legislative and executive bodies, its own Secretariat, and its own budget, but they work with the United Nations and with each other through the co-ordinating machinery of the United Nations Economic and Social Council. The sole exception to this pattern is the International Atomic Energy Agency (IAEA). It reports annually to the General Assembly and, as appropriate, to the Security Council and to the Economic and Social Council. As of June 1961, thirteen other inter-governmental organizations are known as "specialized agencies," a term used in the United Nations Charter; they report annually to the Economic and Social Council.

These thirteen specialized agencies are: the International Labour Organization (ILO); the Food and Agriculture Organization of the United Nations (FAO); the United Nations Educational, Scientific and Cultural Organization (UNESCO); the World Health Organization (WHO); the International Bank for Reconstruction and Development (World Bank); the International Development Association (IDA); the International Finance Corporation (IFC); the International Monetary Fund (FUND); the International Civil Aviation Organization (ICAO); the Universal Postal Union (UPU); the International Telecommunication Union (ITU); the World Meteorological Organization (WMO); and the Inter-Governmental Maritime Consultative Organization (IMCO).

Each specialized agency has agreed to consider any recommendation made to it by the United Nations, and to report to the United Nations, through the Economic and Social Council, on the action taken to give effect to such recommendations. Each specialized agency has further agreed to assist the Security Council in carrying out its decisions for the maintenance or restoration of international peace and security, to assist the Trusteeship Council at the latter's request, and to co-operate with the United Nations in connection with the well-being and development of the peoples of the non-self-governing territories.

In the important field of economic and social development, nine members of the United Nations family work closely together under the United Nations Expanded Programme of Technical Assistance. These nine members are: the United Nations itself, IAEA, ILO, FAO, UNESCO, ICAO, WHO, ITU, and WMO.

This joint undertaking, in operation since 1950, was established by a resolution of the United Nations General Assembly for the purpose of helping under-developed countries to strengthen their national economies. The United Nations and its related agencies also execute, on request, projects authorized by the United Nations Special Fund, a separate body established in 1959 as an expansion of the existing technical assistance activities of the United Nations family.

In addition, certain members also combine their specialized resources in "concerted-action" programmes designed, for example, to improve all phases of life in rural communities, to expand low-cost housing in the rapidly growing cities of underdeveloped countries, and to develop water resources needed for irrigation, power and new industries.

Let us now take a closer look at three of the main organs of the United Nations itself, and consider how the scope and procedures of these bodies can be adapted, with a minimum of distortion, to meet the exigencies of model session requirements.

The General Assembly

The central and most powerful legislative body of the United Nations is the General Asembly. It is composed of all member states. Each member is entitled to send five delegates to the Assembly. It may aslo send five alternate delegates and as many technical advisers as it wishes.

The Assembly's decisions are framed as "recommendations" or "requests" addressed to member states, the other organs, or the inter-governmental agencies related to the United Nations. While these recommendations are not binding, they have the moral force of the majority of the world's governments behind them.

FUNCTIONS AND POWERS

The General Assembly has the right to discuss all matters within the scope of the Charter. The Asembly's powers are qualified only with respect to a dispute or situation on which the Security Council is taking action, in which case the Assembly may discuss but not act. However, under the "Uniting for Peace" resolution adopted by the General Assembly in November 1950, if the Security Council fails to act on a threat of peace, breach of peace or aggression because of a "veto," the Assembly can meet at once and recommend action to the member states.

The Security Council, the Economic and Social Council, the Trusteeship Council, and the Secretary-General submit annual and special reports to the Assembly. The Assembly in effect supervises the work of all other organs of the United Nations by reviewing these reports or by itself taking the initiative.

The Assembly elects the non-permanent members of the Security Council, all members of the Economic and Social Council, and the elective members of the Trusteeship Council. On the recommendation of the Security Council, it appoints the Secretary-General. The Assembly and the Security Council, voting independently, elect the judges of the International Court of Justice. New member nations are admitted to the United Nations by the General Assembly on the recommendation of the Security Council.

VOTING

Each member of the General Assembly has one vote and all votes are equal. Decisions on important questions are made by a two-thirds majority of the members present and voting. as defined in Article 18 of the Charter, these questions include recommendations concerning international peace and security, election of members of the Councils, admission of members, trusteeship questions and budgetary matters. On other questions, it is by a simple majority. As a matter of interest, it may be noted that the vast majority of the Assembly's decisions have been made by the affirmative vote of two-thirds or more of the members and that, with comparatively few exceptions, the question of the application of Article 18 has not ben raised or discussed in connection with the voting.

SESSIONS

The Assembly meets once a year in regular session beginning on the third Tuesday in September. It may also hold special sessions and emergency special sessions at the request of the Security Council or of a majority of United Nations members. As of March 1961, two special sessions have been held, both on the Palestine question, and four emergency special sessions, two on the Middle East, one on Hungary and one on the situation in the Republic of the Congo (Leopoldville).

ORGANIZATION

The General Assembly deals with its work through seven main committees on which all members have the right to be represented. These committees and their responsibilities are:

First Committee: Political and security questions, including the regulation of armaments.

Special Political Committee (to share the work of the First Committee) .

Second Committee: Economic and financial questions.

Third Committee: Social, humanitarian and cultural questions.

Fourth Committee: Trusteeship questions, including those relating to Non-Self-Governing Territories.

Fifth Committee: Administrative and budgetary questions.

Sixth Committee: Legal questions.

In addition, the General Committee meets frequently during a session to supervise the runing of the Assembly's work. It is composed of the President, the thirteen Vice-Presidents of the Assembly and the Chairmen of the seven Main Committees. The Credentials Committee, appointed by the President at each session, verifies the credentials of representatives.

The General Assembly as a rule refers most of the questions on its agenda to one of the Main Committees, to a joint committee, or to an *ad hoc* committee specially established to consider the question. These committees then submit proposals for approval to a plenary meeting of the whole Assembly. Voting in committees and sub-committees is by simple majority. Questions not referred to a committee are dealt with by the Assembly itself in plenary meetings.

SUGGESTIONS FOR MODEL GENERAL ASSEMBLY SESSIONS

The basic elements involved in organizing model sessions of the General Assembly have already been discussed in detail in previous sections of this handbook and can readily be located under relevant headings. Thus, only a few notes, chiefly by way of summary, are given below:

(1) Organizers would be well-advised not to attempt to hold model sessions of the General Assembly until some experience has been gained through the conduct of meetings of United Nations bodies with smaller membership and more concentrated subject-matter, such as the Security Council.

(2) As a first venture, a model Assembly might well be limited to one plenary meeting, with only one main topic on the agenda in addition to words of welcome and a keynote speech.

(3) Whatever the size and scope of the model session, its agen-

da in final form should be established well in advance by the Organizing Committee and circulated to the participants. This procedure permits time for careful study and preparation on the part of each delegation. Without such advance preparation, the educational value of the model session will be largely lost.

(4) As an aid to organizers, an annotated list of suggested agenda items for model Assembly sessions is issued each year by the United Nations Office of Public Information and can be obtained free on request from the nearest United Nations Information Centre or from United Nations Headquarters, New York.

(5) Because of the difficulty of running very large sessions effectively, it is suggested that each participating group be invited to send not more than four delegates and a faculty advisor to a model session. If this is not done, the sheer size of the meeting tends to become in itself a major pre-occupation.

(6) From the above suggestion, it follows that the model Assembly should deal with its work in plenary meetings and not more than four committees. Usually these should be the First Committee, combining the actual Assembly's First and Special Political Committees; the Second Committee; the Third Committee; and the Fourth Committee.

The allocation of agenda items to committees should be made in advance by the Organizing Committee. It should be added that most of the questions dealt with in actual practice by the Assembly's Fifth Committee (Administrative and Budgetary) and Sixth Committee (Legal) are too specialized to be well suited to most model sessions. It should also be noted that it is usually advisable in model sessions for the Organizing Committee to take the place of the actual Assembly's General Committee and Credentials Committee.

(7) As indicated in previous chapters, the Secretary-General, the President of the General Assembly, the Committee chairmen and the rapporteurs should be appointed by the Organizing Committee and not elected by the participants.

(8) In making up the model session programme, it is customary for events, such as the admission of new members and the "general debate" which in actual practice would be spread over several meetings, to be foreshortened to suit the time available to the model session. This is inevitable and only requires realistic advance planning on the part of the Organizing Committee and

careful adherence to the established time-schedule during the meeting itself for the session to run smoothly.

(9) Modified rules of procedure for a model General Assembly session are given in Appendix IV of this handbook. These should be adjusted by the Organizing Committee to suit the particular requirements which may obtain in the local situation.

(10) Because the time available in model sessions is very limited, voting in plenary and in committee meetings should be kept to a minimum, with roll-call votes used only sparingly, if indeed at all. Also, time should not be wasted in procedural wrangles.

(11) It has become the custom in some large-scale model sessions to hold simultaneously meetings of the General Assembly, the Security Council, the Trusteeship Council and the Economic and Social Council. Some sessions include other bodies such as the International Court of Justice, the Disarmament Commission, the Human Rights Commission, and others. These concurrent sessions are undertaken in order to accommodate the large number of students who wish to participate in the session. This practice is definitely not recommended, for two main reasons: (a) the larger the number of people and the more organs involved in a model session, the more difficult it becomes to run well; and (b) with few exceptions, such concurrent meetings of major organs are, not held in actual United Nations practice because so many questions require referral from one United Nations body to another for further action, study or approval as successive stages in their consideration are reached.

In general, therefore, it is suggested that the Organizing Committee plan to portray in a model session only one organ at a time, reducing—if need be—the number of participants involved. The most likely exception to this general rule would be for model meetings of the Security Council to be held during the course of a model General Assembly session, since under the actual provisions of the Charter, the agenda of these two bodies could not be allowed to overlap.

The Security Council

Under the Charter, members of the United Nations have conferred on the Security Council the primary responsibility for maintaining international peace and security. For this purpose, they have agreed that it is to act for all of them and that they will accept and carry out its decisions.

The Security Council is composed of eleven members of the United Nations. Five of these are permanent members — China, France, the Union of Soviet Socialist Republics, the United Kingdom and the United States of America. Six are non-permanent members, elected by the General Assembly for two-year terms. Members are not eligible for immediate re-election.[1] Each Council member has one representative.

Any member of the United Nations which is not a member of the Council may participate, without vote, in any discussion in the Council if the Council considers that the interests of that member are especially affected.

Any state, whether a member of the United Nations or not, which is a party to a dispute being considered by the Council, must be invited to participate, without vote in the discussions.

FUNCTIONS AND POWERS

The first responsibility of the Security Council is to maintain international peace and security. The General Assembly, any member of the United Nations, or the Secretary-General of the United Nations can bring to the Council's attention any matter that threatens peace. A non-member state can bring a dispute in which it is involved before the Council provided it accepts in advance the Charter obligations for peaceful settlement.

The first action of the Council when a complaint is brought before it is usually to recommend that the parties concerned try themselves — if they have not already done so — to reach agreement, by using the Charter methods of negotiation, mediation, conciliation or judicial settlement. In some cases, it has been necessary for the Council itself to undertake investigation and mediation.

Where disputes lead to actual hostilities, the Council's first concern is to secure a cease-fire. This was the case in Palestine, Kashmir and Indonesia. If a call by the Security Council to stop fighting goes unheed, then the Council can decide what measures should be taken to enforce its decision. It may, for example,

---

1. The non-permanent members (as of June 1961) are: Ceylon, Chile, Ecuador, Liberia, Turkey and the United Arab Republic.

call for the interruption of communications or the breaking off of diplomatic relations with the offending country, and, finally, it may take military action. Such decisions of the Council are binding on all United Nations members.

The Security Council has other duties apart from its main task of maintaining peace and security. It recommends to the General Assembly which countries should be admitted to membership in the United Nations. On the basis of the Security Council's recommendation, the General Assembly appoints the Secretary-General and, together with the General Assembly, the Council elects the judges of the International Court of Justice. Finally, the Security Council approves trusteeship agreements for areas which are designated as "strategic;" so far there is one such area — the Trust Territory of the Pacific Islands.

VOTING

Each member of the Security Council has one vote. Decisions on procedural matters are made by an affirmative vote of any seven members. Decisions on substantive matters are made by an affirmative vote of seven members, including the concurring votes of the five permanent members, except that any member must abstain from voting in decisions concerning the pacific settlement of a dispute to which it is a party.[1] A negative vote by a permanent member on a matter of substance is popularly referred to as a "veto."

SESSIONS

Because of the urgent character of its work, the Security Council is so organized as to be able to function continuously, and a representative of each of its members must be present at all times at the Headquarters of the United Nations. The Council may meet elsewhere than at Headquarters if it considers this advisable.

ORGANIZATION

The presidency of the Council is held monthly in turn by the

---

1. For detailed discussion of voting procedures in the Security Council, with case histories, the serious student is referred to the *Reportoire of the Practice of the Security Council, 1946-1951*, New York, United Nations, (1954) pp. 25-51; *Supplement 1952-1955* (1957), pp. 7-12; *Supplement 1956-1958* (1959), pp. 60-77.

member states in English alphabetical order. The Council decides
its own rules of procedure and may establish what subsidiary
organs it considers necessary.. The most important of these subsidiary bodies is the Disarmament Commission, etablished by the
General Assembly on 11 January 1952, under the Security Council. The Disarmament Commission is composed of all member
states of the United Nations. The Security Council also makes
use from time to time of *ad hoc* committees and commissions, e.g.
the United Nations Commission for Indonesia, and the United
Nations Representative for India and Pakistan.

A word should be added concerning the Military Staff Committee. In order to enable the United Nations to take urgent enforce-
ment action, the Charter provides that member countries should
ear-mark contingents of their armed forces for this purpose on
plans to be worked out by a Military Staff Committee of the
Security Council. Since its establishment in 1946, this Committee
has each year submitted a report of its activities which has been
included in the annual report of the Security Council to the
General Assembly. However, ever since the Committee reported
to the Security Council in 1948 its inability to agree either on
the question of the over-all strength and composition of the
armed forces or on the future work of the Committee, no further
progress has been made by the Committee on matters of substance.

SUGGESTIONS FOR MODEL SECURITY COUNCIL SESSIONS

(1) The Security Council can be portrayed particularly well
in a small model session held within a single class or school, both
because of the limited size of its membership and also since at
each of its meetings, or series of successive meetings, only one
major question is usually discussed. A further practical advantage
is that the verbatim records of the Security Council are issued
in separate sections which can be purchased singly or severally
as needed to cover the whole course of the Council's action on
the particular question concerned. As indicated in the selected
list of United Nations documents and publications given in Appendix VI, the cost of these sections is very modest and thus
the important advantage of using the verbatim records of the
Council to prepare for the model session can usually be gained,
even on a very small budget.

(2) A model Security Council might hold only one session and limit its programme to include brief words of welcome to the audience, the discussion of a single question by the Council, and a keynote or closing address by a distinguished speaker. A larger model session might function for one full day. In this case, registration could begin at 9 a.m. and the first session could start at 10 a.m. The Council could have two agenda items before it: one for the morning session and one for the afternoon session. A box luncheon at 12:30 or 1:00 p.m. might feature a guest speaker, followed by a question and answer period. The afternoon session could then move on to the second agenda item, and close at approximately 5 p.m. with a brief critique. Tea and a social hour could then follow, if desired and convenient; however, it is not essential.

(3) Programmes such as these could involve from twenty to thirty or more participants, depending on how the session is planned. In a day-long session, there could be, for example, two representatives for each of the eleven member countries on the Security Council, with one serving as delegate and one as advisor for the morning session. These roles could then be reversed in the afternoon session. In addition, the question or questions decided on for the agenda might involve the participation in the Council's deliberation of some non-members of the Council, in which case representatives of such countries would need also to be allowed for. In this connexion it should be noted that in actual practice the participation, without vote, of non-members of the Council in its deliberations is by no means uncommon and sometimes includes as many as five or more countries.

(4) In actual practice, the Presidency of the Council is held monthly in turn by each of its members. However, some model sessions prefer to have the Organizing Committee appoint a presiding officer who is not one of the delegates; all of the delegates are then free from the added responsibility of conducting the session and can concentrate on representing a member state.

(5) It will be necessary to provide for a Secretary-General, and also for one or more small working committees to take charge of practical arrangements, such as sending out invitations to the participants and audience, ensuring that the meeting-room is available and attractively decorated, and printing or mimeographing programmes. The Secretary-General should, of course,

sit at the Council table. Depending on the question concerned, he may be called upon to make an oral or written report to the Council or he may intervene at times in the debate.

(6) In establishing the agenda of the model session, it is very important that the questions selected should be matters which have actually come before the Security Council for consideration so that the proceedings can be firmly rooted in reality. If this crucial step is not taken, the educational value of the model session will be largely lost. It is important also that the question or questions selected should be limited to those on which the Council has already reached a decision and on which the verbatim records are issued and available. It cannot be stressed too strongly that it is distinctly unwise to select for discussion at a model session highly complex questions which are still under active consideration from one day to the next in the Security Council. This mistake is often made by model sessions in the effort to keep pace with the current headlines in the world's newspapers. It should be recognized clearly that adequate and accurate documentation can seldom be obtained by model sessions under such circumstances. The result of emphasis on topical currency is likely to be added confussion concerning the issues, rather than deepened understanding of the work of the United Nations.

(7) The annual *Report of the Security Council to the General Assembly* provides an excellent source of suggestions for suitable agenda items for model Security Council sessions. This report, which covers the period from 16 July of the previous year to 15 July of the current year, forms part of the *Official Records* of each regular annual session of the General Assembly and is always printed as Supplement No. 2. The agenda for each meeting of the Security Council is found also in the verbatim *Official Records of the Security Council* itself. These are generally published quarterly unless the records are so extensive as to require publication more frequently. It should be noted also that the monthly *United Nations Review* covers fully the meetings of the Council as they occur; it includes the texts of resolutions adopted and a complete list of the documents concerned. Except in the case of completely new items, the historical background of the question in the United Nations will be given in summary in *Everyman's United Nations* and more fully in the annual volumes of

the *United Nations Yearbook*. It should be added that, if feasible, it is usually also very helpful to seek the advice of the Director of the nearest United Nations Information Centre, or other qualified experts, on the choice of topics before a final decision on the agenda is reached.

(8) Modified rules of procedure for use in model Security Council sessions are given in Appendix V of this handbook. These can be adapted to suit local requirements, particularly in respect to such matters as the language or languages in which the model session may find it best to conduct its proceedings. Again it should be stressed the model session should focus its attention squarely on the substance of the question being considered and not on points of procedure.

(9) Because of their special character, the actual practices followed by the Security Council in respect of the participation of non-members of the Council in its deliberations may be worth noting. In most cases, the countries concerned have submitted written applications to the Security Council to participate in its discussions and such requests have usually been granted. In a few cases, the Council has initiated the invitation. Such invitations may be issued to member states whose interests are considered by the Council to be specially affected, and to members bringing to the attention of the Council a situation which is thought to endanger international peace and security. After the adoption of the agenda, the President of the Council invites the approved non-members to take places at the Council table. Once at the table, these non-members take part in the discussion of the question under consideration in the same manner as the members of the Council, except for two important limitations. First, of course, such non-members may not vote. Secondly, while a member so invited may submit resolutions and draft resolutions to the Council, such proposals can be put to a vote only at the request of a Council member.

(10) The practice of the Security Council is to vote by show of hands, and, when so doing, to ask for the votes of those in favour, those against and those abstaining. In the record of votes, members are also identified as not having participated or as having been absent. In elections, the voting is conducted by secret ballot. For secret ballots in connexion with the election of the Secretary-General, two ballots have been used to enable the

tellers to distinguish the votes of the permanent and those of the elected members. However, elections will usually not concern model sessions of the Security Council. With respect to the much-discussed veto, the most practical course would be for participants in model sessions to study carefully the Security Council verbatim records, including the votes taken, on the questions to be discussed at the model session and then to vote exactly as did the member state concerned. This would include the use of the veto if it actually was used. In sum, the veto would not seem to pose any specific difficulties if the agenda followed by the model session includes only items which have actually been discussed in the Security Council and for which the verbatim records are available.

The Economic and Social Council (ECOSOC)

The Economic and Social Council, one of the six main organs of the United Nations, is the body responsible, under the authority of the General Assembly, for carrying out the functions of the United Nations with regard to international co-operation for economic and social development.

As set forth in Article 55 of the Charter, the objectives of the United Nations in this field are to promote: (a) higher standards of living, full employment, and conditions of economic and social progress and development; (b) solutions of international economic, social, health, and related problems; (c) international cultural and educational co-operation; and (d) universal respect for, and observance of, human rights and fundamental freedoms for all. These activities are expressly aimed at "the creation of conditions of stability and well-being which are necessary for peaceful and friendly relations among nations."

COMPOSITION

The Council consists of eighteen members of the United Nations elected by a two-thirds majority of the General Assembly.[1] Six are elected each year for three year terms. Members may be

1. As of June 1961, the members of the Council are: Afghanistan, Bulgaria, New Zealand, Spain, United States, Venezuela (until 1962); Brazil, Denmark, Japan, Poland, USSR, United Kingdom (until 1963); El Salvador, Ethiopia, France, Jordan, Uruguay and Italy (until 1964).

re-elected immediately and often are. Each member of the Council is represented by one delegate.

The Council may invite any member state not a member of the Council to participate, without the right to vote, in discussions of any matter of particular concern to that member. The invitation is extended by the President, with the agreement of the Council, either at the request of the member state concerned, or at the request of a Council member, or on his own initiative.

Representatives of the specialized agencies regularly are invited to attend the meetings of the Council and its commissions and committees, and to participate "in consultative capacity," but without a vote, in the discussion of any matter of particular concern to the agency. Representatives may also submit proposals regarding such items, which may be put to a vote on the request of a Council member.

Non-governmental organizations which have been admitted to consultative status by ECOSOC may send observers to the public meetings of the Council and its commissions. Those admitted to Categories A and B may also present their views on matters with which they are concerned in written and oral statements to the Council. As of June 1961, categories A and B include 129 organizations which have a basic interest and special competence in all or most of the Council's activities. An additional 205 organizations are on a register for consultation on matters relevant to their particular interests.

FUNCTIONS AND POWERS

The Council makes or initiates studies and reports on international economic, social, cultural, educational, health and related matters. It makes recommendations on such matters to the General Assembly, to the members of the United Nations, and to the specialized agencies concerned. It also makes recommendations for the purpose of promoting respect for and observance of human rights.

The Council prepares draft conventions for submission to the General Assembly on matters within its competence and calls international conferences on such matters. It enters into agreements with the specialized agencies, defining the terms of their relations with the United Nations, subject to the approval of the General Assembly. It makes arrangements for consultation with relevant nongovernmental organizations. Finally, with the approval of the General Assembly, it obtains reports from member nations on steps taken to give effect to its recommendations, and those of the Assembly, on matters which fall within its competence.

VOTING

Each member of the Council has one vote. Decisions are made by a simple majority of the members present and voting. The normal method of voting in the Council is by show of hands. Only a few decisions have been made by roll-call vote. Elections are decided by secret ballot. A frequent exception to this rule is the election by acclamation of the President and the two Vice-Presidents of the Council.

If a vote is equally divided on matters other than elections, the proposal is regarded as rejected. In the case of elections, further ballots are held.

SESSIONS

The Council normally meets in regular session twice a year; in a spring session at United Nations Headquarters, New York, and in a summer session held usually for about five weeks at the Palais des Nations, Geneva, beginning early in July. Special sessions may also be held if required.

ORGANIZATION

The Council adopts its own rules of procedure. It elects its President and two Vice-Presidents from among its own members, who serve for a year. It also establishes such subsidiary bodies as it considers necessary.

Since its responsibilities are so broad in scope, the Council itself is mainly a central policy-making and co-ordinating organ. Most of the operational work falling within its purview is done by the autonomous intergovernmental agencies related to the United Nations, and by the Council's subsidiary bodies, including its regional and functional commissions, standing and *ad hoc* committees, and several special bodies, such as the United Nations Children's Fund (UNICEF).

The Council has established four regional economic commissions, each with its headquarters within the region concerned. These are: the Economic Commission for Europe (ECE, Geneva) ; Asia and the Far East (ECAFE), Bangkok) ; Latin America (ECLA, Santiago) ; and Africa (ECA, Addis Ababa). These commissions study the economic problems of their regions and recommend courses of action to governments on matters concerned with economic development. The commissions also work closely with each other and with other relevant bodies in their areas to promote agricultural and industrial production and to increase trade both among the countries of the region and with the rest of the world. The commissions generally hold plenary meetings within their regions once a year and report annually to ECOSOC at its summer session.

The functional commissions of ECOSOC undertake studies and make recommendations to the Council in their special fields. There are seven of these commissions: the Statistical Commission, the Population Commission, the Social Commission, the Commission on Human Rights (including the Sub-Commission on Prevention of Discrimination and Protection of Minorities), the Commission on the Status of Women, the Commission on Narcotic Drugs; and the Commission on International Commodity Trade.

Although the Council in plenary meeting usually initiates debates on major issues, most agenda items are referred to one of the Council's standing committees (Economic, Social, Co-ordination, Technical Assistance, Industrial Development, Programme of Conferences, and Non-governmental Organizations) for discussion and recommendations. The first three of these are committees of the whole. The Technical Assistance Committee includes the eighteen members of ECOSOC, and six additional members elected by the Council from other member states of the United Nations and its related agencies. The recommendations of these committees are usually adopted by the Council as prescribed.

From time to time, the Council establishes such *ad hoc* committees as it considers necessary.

Suggestions for Model ECOSOC Sessions

(1) The available evidence indicates that the Economic and Social Council is portrayed in model sessions far less often than

the General Assembly or the Security Council. However, from an educational point of view, model sessions of ECOSOC would seem potentially to have special merit for several reasons: First, if they are well planned and conducted, such sessions could provide an effective means of focussing attention on the important work of the United Nations family in the field of international co-operation for economic and social advancement. These activities seldom make headlines in the world's newspapers and are generally much less well-known and understood than the political work of the United Nations. Secondly, the direct relevance of specific areas of the work of the Council and the specialized agencies to subjects already in the curricula of some secondary schools, and most colleges and universities and teacher-training institutions, could be put to use in preparing for model sessions of ECOSOC. Intensive reading and analysis of relevant reports and discussions of the United Nations and its related agencies would considerably enrich classroom study in such fields as economics, sociology and social work, education, health and agriculture, among many others. Finally, the varied nature of the Council's responsibilities would make possible a considerable measure of flexibility in planning the agenda of a model session of ECOSOC to suit the special subject and geographic interests of participants concerned.

(2) To avoid confusion, it is essential to keep the basic structure of a model session of ECOSOC clear and simple. Thus, organizers should decide to hold a model session which portrays the whole Council at work in plenary meeting, or one which presents a subsidiary body in action, such as one of the functional or regional commissions — but only one body at a time. In sum, concurrent meetings of several different bodies should not be attempted. This procedure need not detract from the interest of the meeting, since the agenda of the model session might well include carefully prepared five-minute reports on the work of one or more of the various related bodies as a special feature.

(3) As in well-run model sessions of any United Nations body, the agenda in final form should be drawn up by the Organizing Committee and circulated to the participants well in advance to allow time for careful preparation.

(4) To keep the model session proceedings firmly rooted in reality, the agenda items should be selected from among subjects

of major importance which have actually been discussed at recent sessions of the body concerned and on which sufficient documentation is readily available.

(5) Excellent sources of agenda items are the annual *Report of the Economic and Social Council,* which is presented each year to the regular session of the General Assembly and is always printed as Supplement No. 3 to the *Official Records;* and the monthly *United Nations Review,* particularly the issues which appear immediately following the close of the two regular half-yearly sessions of the Council. These usually appear in May and September. In addition to articles which review the work of the sessions, the "United Nations Digest" section of the *Review* summarizes the action taken on each agenda item and lists the relevant documents by number. It should also be noted that in advance of each session, an "Annotated Provisional Agenda" which providing useful background information on the prospective agenda items is issued by the United Nations Office of Public Information in the form of a mimeographed press release. This press release can be obtained free on request from the nearest United Nations Information Centre. If feasible, it is usually helpful to consult the Director of the Information Centre or other qualified experts on the choice of topics before a final decision on the agenda is reached.

(6) Several factors should determine the number of participants to be invited: the particular body to be presented; the physical facilities available; the length of the session; and the agenda, including the number of special features. A model session of ECOSOC itself could very well hold one plenary meeting only and limit its agenda to the discussion of one main item, such as a review of the current world economic situation. This topic is, in fact, always a major highlight of the summer session of the Council. In this case, it would be necessary to have on hand the eighteen members of the Council, the President of the Council, and the Secretary-General, who always makes a statement introducing this item. The President of the Council may be one of the Council Members, or he may be appointed by the Organizing Committee. A brief welcome to the audience and a keynote or closing speech could complete the programme. A programme of this nature could be held during an afternoon or evening.

A programme lasting a full day might include such special

features as brief reports from participants acting as the Executive Secretaries of the four regional economic commissions on outstanding current trends and developments in their respective areas. It might also include brief comments from participants invited as representatives from relevant specialized agencies, in order to emphasize the interdependence of economic and social development in such fields as health and education. Short statements might also be made by "observers" from one or more relevant nongovernmental organizations. As a change of pace, one or two carefully selected short films might be shown to convey a vivid impression of some of the typical field projects operating under the United Nations programme of technical assistance.

An alternate possibility would be to have two main agenda items: one for the morning session and one for the afternoon session. One item might be a review of the world social situation. In this case, special features might include brief prepared reports from one or more of the functional commissions of ECOSOC, such as human rights, the status of women or population questions. A speaker from the Secretariat of one of the specialized agencies might be found to discuss relevant aspects of the work of the body concerned, such as UNESCO's efforts to aid its member states to develop their educational systems, or the Freedom-from-Hunger Campaign of FAO.

(7) Plenary meetings of each of the four regional economic commissions could be well portrayed in model sessions, particularly in countries located within the area covered by the commission concerned.[1] Care should be taken to ensure that the past accomplishments and current activities of the commission are discussed in relation to the basic economic problems and progress of the region, so that the practical realities of international co-operation for economic development can be more fully understood by both the participants and the audience.

As special features of such meetings, it might be of interest to have possibly by one of the officials concerned a report presented on a specific project of major importance to a region. One ex-

---

1. For a detailed discussion of how meetings of ECE are organized, see: L. Kopelmanes, "The technique of international conferences and the experience of the Economic Commission for Europe", *International Social Science Bulletin* (UNESCO), vol. V, No. 2 (1953), pp. 343-360.

ample might be the Lower Mekong River Basin development scheme — "the TVA of Asia" — which is intended to aid the economic development of the four countries involved: Cambodia, Laos, Thailand and Vietnam. An example drawn from Latin America, might the many-sided Central American Economic Integration Programme. An outline map large enough to be plainly seen by the audience will add considerably to the teaching value of the presentation.

The key documents for study in preparing for such meetings include the yearly *Economic Survey* of the region issued by each of the commissions, the commissions' quarterly *Economic Bulletins* which report current developments, and the annual report made by the Executive Secretary of each of the four commissions to the summer session of ECOSOC. Accounts of the meetings of the commissions are published regularly in the monthly *United Nations Review*.

In planning model sessions of the commissions, it is necessary to check the current membership of the body concerned, because it may change from time to time. This is particularly true of ECA, which originally had several trust and non-self-governing territories as associate members. These have since become full members upon reaching independence.

Each of the regional commissions also has a number of subsidiary bodies, which deal with such subjects as trade, inland transport, housing, electric power and the like. However, the meetings of such bodies are usually highly specialized and technical in content and, in general, would not be suitable for presentation in model sessions.

(8) The importance of careful study by each participant of the basic documents relevant to the items placed on the agenda of the model session can hardly be over-stressed. While this comment applies generally to model sessions of any United Nations body, it is particularly crucial in the case of ECOSOC, since discussion of virtually all of the subjects considered by the Council in plenary sessions are based squarely on the facts and analyses contained in the major reports and studies placed before the Council for policy decisions. Moreover, from the point of view of education, such documents as the annual *World Economic Survey*, the yearly regional economic surveys, and the biennial *Report on the World Social Situation* provide basic information

and insights which the serious student of economic and social affairs will find most rewarding to master. These studies also provide the indispensable factual basis of international action for the common welfare of mankind.

Summaries of the studies noted above appear regularly in the *United Nations Review*. However, it is suggested that whenever possible the full report itself, rather than a summary, should be read.

It should be added that in actual practice the work of ECOSOC is greatly facilitated by the presentation of carefully prepared statements by the Secretary-General in introducing the general debate on major questions. It is also greatly facilitated by the written and oral reports presented by the Council's regional and functional commissions and by the specialized agencies. This practice is here suggested as a very useful means of adding substantially to the informational content of the model session. Obviously, such reports should be prepared with great care in advance by the participants concerned so that the time of the audience and Council members will not be wasted.

(9) The meetings of ECOSOC are conducted under its own rules of procedure which are available in published form.[1] They may be purchased from sales agents or consulted in depository libraries and should be adapted as necessary to meet local requirements. The Council has also drawn up and published a set of official rules of procedure for its functional commissions.[2] Each of the four regional economic commissions has adopted its own rules of procedure, which can be obtained free of cost on request to the commission concerned.

In point of fact, it is interesting to note that in the meetings of the Council and its subsidiary bodies, reference is rarely made to the rules of procedure. Instead, practical requirements rather than the letter of the law govern the conduct of meetings, the relations of delegations with one another, and the Council's relation with the Secretariat, and with the representatives of other international governmental organizations. Model sessions should also follow this sensible practice.

---

1. *Rules of Procedure of the Economic and Social Council* (E F S R), 58.I.3, 30 p., $0.25, 1/9, 1 Sw. fr.

2. *Rules of Procedure of the Functional Commissions of the Economic and Social Council* (E F S), 53.I.22, 20 p., $0.15, 1/-, 0.50 Sw. fr.

(10) The rules of procedure of the Council and those of its subsidiary bodies provide that decisions shall be made by a simple majority of the members present and voting. In actual practice, however, the tendency in the Council and its bodies is to seek unanimity in adopting resolutions on substantive questions. This tendency is particularly marked in the case of the four regional economic commissions.

It should further be noted that if a vote is equally divided on matters other than elections, the proposal is regarded as rejected. It is thus clear that in the Council and its related bodies, the basic objective sought is not the shadow of voting victories but rather the substance of concerted action freely undertaken by sovereign member states for the common welfare of the international community.

CHAPTER VIII

Model Sessions of the
General Conference of UNESCO

THE UNITED NATIONS Educational, Scientific and Cultural Organization (UNESCO) is one of the thirteen Specialized Agencies which work with the United Nations, with the International Atomic Energy Agency, and with each other, under the general co-ordinating authority of the United Nations Economic and Social Council. This relationship is illustrated in the chart in Appendix VIII.

Each of the Agencies of the United Nations system has its own clearly defined areas of activity in the field of economic and social development. The purpose and tasks of UNESCO are stated in Article I of its Constitution:

"1. The purpose of the Organization is to contribute to peace and security by promoting collaboration among the nations through education, science and culture in order to further universal respect for justice, for the rule of law and for the human rights and fundamental freedoms which are affirmed for the peoples of the world, without distinction of race, sex, language or religion, by the Charter of the United Nations."

"2. To realize this purpose the Organization will:

   (a) collaborate in the work of advancing the mutual knowledge and understanding of peoples, through all means of mass communication and to that end recommend such international agreements as may be necessary to promote the free flow of ideas by word and image;

   (b) give fresh impulse to popular education and to the spread of culture; by collaborating with Members, at their request, in the development of educational activities;

by instituting collaboration among the nations to advance the ideal of equality of educational opportunity without regard to race, sex or any distinctions, economic or social;

by suggesting educational methods best suited to prepare the children of the world for the responsibilities of freedom;

(c) maintain, increase and diffuse knowledge;

by assuring the conservation and protection of the world's inheritance of books, works of art and monuments of history and science, and recommending to the nations concerned the necessary international conventions;

by encouraging co-operation among the nations in all branches of intellectual activity, including the international exchange of persons active in the fields of education, science and culture and the exchange of publications, objects of artistic and scientific interest and other materials of information; by initiating methods of international co-operation calculated to give the people of all countries access to the printed and published materials produced by any of them."

Activities of UNESCO

The programme of activities submitted every two years to the General Conference is the result of joint planning and review by the Secretariat and the Executive Board, in consultation with member states, the United Nations and other specialized agencies. International nongovernmental organizations collaborating with UNESCO are also consulted about proposed activities in their fields of competence.

The Organization's programme can be broken down into eleven priority areas:

a. Development of international co-operation among specialists;
b. Improvement of documentation;
c. Development of school and higher education;
d. Development of out-of-school education;

  e. Aid to research in the various branches of science;
  f. Application of the social sciences to social problems;
  g. Preservation of the cultural heritage of mankind;
  h. Mutual appreciation of cultural values;
  i. Free flow of information and improvement of communication media;
  j. The training of specialists abroad;
  k. Implementation of human rights.

In 1956, the General Conference approved one large-scale project in each of the fields of education, science and culture, with the aim of achieving large-scale results within a given period in the solution of important problems. These major projects are: the extension of primary education in Latin America through the training of teachers; scientific research in arid lands; and the development of mutual appreciation of Eastern and Western Cultural Values.

Further large-scale projects were launched by the General Conference in 1960, notably projects for educational development in Africa, for the development of primary education in Asia and Arab-speaking countries, and for oceanographic research.

In addition to its own regular budget, UNESCO receives funds under the United Nations Expanded Programme of Technical Assistance for the supply of expert missions, training equipment and fellowships for study abroad, in response to requests from member states approved by the Technical Assistance Board.

The Organization also administers projects financed by the Special Fund, which has been established by the United Nations to extend further assistance towards the economic advancement of the less developed countries. Its object is to facilitate the establishment of basic machinery essential to economic development as a prerequisite to productive capital investments.

Also, within the Programme of Participation in the Activities of Member States, financed from UNESCO's own budget, countries can request specialist services, equipment and fellowships for projects concentrating, for example, on social or intellectual activities. The Participation Programme is designed to fill gaps in fields of activity where neither Technical Assistance nor the Special Fund are authorized to operate, i.e., in projects not directly concerned with economic progress.

National Commissions

An important feature of UNESCO is that its Constitution calls for the creation within each member state of national co-operating bodies, or National Commissions. Most member states have set up such commissions, broadly representative of their respective governments and of the principal national organizations interested in education, science and culture. Their main purpose is to associate interested national bodies with UNESCO's work, to advise their respective governments and delegations to the General Conference on matters of concern to the Organization, and to act as liaison agencies with the Secretariat and with each other. Because of their broad representation, the National Commissions can serve as instruments to bring to life UNESCO's work and purposes within each member state.

Structure of UNESCO

UNESCO includes three organs: the General Conference (described below in some detail), the Executive Board, and the Secretariat.

The *Executive Board* is responsible to the General Conference of Member States for seeing that the programme it has approved is carried out as completely and efficiently as possible. The Board consists of 24 members, elected by the General Conference from among its delegates, each of whom represents the government of the state of which he is the national.

The Executive Board meets in regular session at least twice a year. Its task is to act on behalf of the General Conference between sessions, mainly to supervise the execution of the programme and the general operation of the Organization, and also to prepare the work of the next session of the General Conference and, in particular, to examine the proposed programme and budget prepared by the Director-General.

The *Secretariat*, which has its Headquarters in Paris, has an international staff recruited from UNESCO member states. Some staff members are employed in regional field offices and many technical assistance experts are recruited annually for mission assignments in different countries.

The Secretariat is responsible for the execution of UNESCO's programme as a whole. At its head is the Director-General, chief

administrative officer of the Organization, who is appointed by
the General Conference for a term of six years.

The General Conference

UNESCO's General Conference consists of representatives of
member states of the Organization. Each Government may appoint up to five delegates who are selected in consultation with
National Commissions or with educational, scientific and cultural bodies. Delegations may include up to five alternate delegates, and as many advisers and experts as are deemed necessary.

FUNCTIONS: The General Conference determines the policies
and the main lines of work of the Organization. It takes decisions on the programmes submitted to it by the Executive Board,
votes the budget for putting them into action, and adopts recommendations and conventions for submission to member states'
Governments. It is responsible for selection of the Executive
Board, appointment of the Director-General, and admission of
new member states.

SESSIONS: The General Conference meets in ordinary session
every two years. In addition to member states' delegations, the
United Nations and other Specialized Agencies are notified of
sessions of the General Conference and are entitled to send representatives; member states of the United Nations which are not
members of UNESCO, appropriate intergovernmental organizations, non-governmental or semi-governmental organizations approved for consultative arrangements with UNESCO are invited
to send observers. Non-self-governing territories can be proposed
by the administering power for associate membership in UNESCO
which gives them the right to make proposals and to take part
in debates of the General Conference.

VOTING: Each member state has one vote in the General Conference and in any of its Commissions, Committees or sub-bodies.

Decisions are made by a simple majority, i.e., a majority of
the members present and voting. Exceptions to this rule requir-
ing a two-thirds majority are: admission of new member states
which are not members of the United Nations; adoption of international conventions for submission to governments of member
states'; admission of observers of nongovernmental organizations
and semi-governmental organizations; amendments to the Consti-

tution; adoption of regulations governing procedure for amendments to the Constitution.

ORGANIZATION AND PROCEDURE: The decisions of the General Conference are framed as resolutions authorizing the programme to be carried out; recommendations to member states, which, like the recommendations made by the United Nations, are not binding but have a moral force; or as international conventions for submission to member states which become legal instruments when ratified by member states.

At the opening of each session of the General Conference delegates establish the committees and commissions which are required to carry out the business of the session. All member states are represented in both the Programme Commission, in which the main discussion of the Organization's activities for the ensuing two years takes place, and in the Administrative Commission, which establishes the budgetary level and carries out the administrative business of the Conference. Both Commissions' reports are represented to the General Conference in plenary session for amendment and approval.

Other Committees are:

(1)   the Credentials Committee which examines the credentials of delegations, representatives and observers and reports immediately to the Conference (9 members);

(2)   the Nominations Committee which submits to the Conference nominations for President and twelve vice-presidents and proposals for the composition of committees and commissions (heads of all member states' delegations);

(3)   the Legal Committee which considers proposals for the amendment of the Constitution or Rules of Procedure and any legal question which may be referred to it by the Conference (15 members);

(4)   the General Committee which deals with time and order of business of plenary meetings, considers requests for new items for the agenda and co-ordinates the work of the General Conference and the various committees and commissions. (President, 12 vice-presidents and chairmen of all committees and commissions).

As indicated above, most of the work of the General Conference is done in the commissions and committees and reported to the plenary sessions. Apart from taking final decisions on these reports, however, the plenary session carries out an important function in holding general debates in which every delegation has the right to set forth its general policy and to express its views about the nature and direction of the Organization's activities.

Organizing a Model Session of Unesco's General Conference

Most of the advice and suggestions concerning model sessions of United Nations bodies given earlier in Chapters IV and VII can be applied or adapted in preparing a model session of a UNESCO General Conference. If all member states are to be represented at the session, in order to ensure a balanced debate, the meeting will inevitably be a large one and, as suggested on page 15, should only be attempted when the organizers have already had some experience with a model meeting of a smaller body, such as the Security Council.

The general rules of procedure (Appendix IV) established for use in model sessions of the United Nations General Assembly might be modified for use in a model session of the General Conference of UNESCO. Alternatively, the official rules of procedure can be found in the UNESCO *Conference Manual* published by the Organization.

The best source of agenda items to be discussed would probably be the printed volume of *Records of the General Conference* published by the Organization after each session. It contains the texts of resolutions and of any conventions and recommendations adopted. It also includes the reports of commissions, committees and working parties. *Proceedings of the General Conference*, also published in printed form after each session, contains verbatim reports of debates in all plenary sessions. These publications are on sale at UNESCO Sales Agents in different countries, or may be consulted in UNESCO Depository Libraries and United Nations Information Centres.

Annotated specimen agenda items considered at the 11th session of the General Conference of UNESCO held in 1960, and the texts of several resolutions adopted by the Conference, are given below.

Annotated Specimen Agenda Items

1. AID TO AFRICAN STATES: EMERGENCY PROGRAMME OF ADDITIONAL
   AID FOR THE DEVELOPMENT OF EDUCATION IN AFRICA

At the 11th Session of the UNESCO General Conference in
1960, following a general debate on the needs of Tropical Africa,
this item was introduced by Yugoslavia, co-sponsored by Nigeria,
Poland, Senegal, Sweden, United Kingdom and the United States
of America. In the earlier debate, which was introduced by a
survey of needs in Africa (11 C/PRG/13), and which culminated
in a general resolution approving an emergency programme for
Africa to be financed from UNESCO's budget and supplemented
by allocations from the Expanded Programme of Technical Assistance and from the United Nations Special Fund, education
had emerged as the vital and urgent need of the region. The
general resolution, which was later adopted by the General Conference (Resolution 1.2322), listed four main purposes: (1)
Construction of educational buildings; (2) Production of teaching aids; (3) Provision of overseas teachers and professors; (4)
Assessment of educational needs.

The new proposal provided for voluntary financial contributions for the four purposes set forth in Resolution 1.2322 as
well as for the operation of a clearing house to publicise financial
and investment needs of the African countries as a means of
promoting multilateral, regional and bi-lateral co-operation
among member states. It was intended to meet the financial and
capital needs for the development of education in Africa, which,
as pointed out in the survey (11 C/PRG/13), could not be met
from UNESCO's budgetary and extra-budgetary resources. A
resolution was approved unanimously by the Programme Commission and later adopted without change by the General Conference (Resolution 1.2323).

TEXT OF RESOLUTION 1.2323

The General Conference,
Noting that the educational needs of the countries of Africa
   are vast and urgent,
Being aware that educational development is a major factor
   and condition precedent for the economic, social and cultural development of those countries,

Being Informed of the needs disclosed in the inquiry carried out by UNESCO in the countries of Africa in 1959 and of the conclusions and recommendations in that connexion adopted by the Meeting of Ministers or Directors of Education of Tropical African countries at Addis Ababa in 1960 (11 C/PRG/1 and 11 C/PRG/13),

Noting with satisfaction the strengthening of UNESCO's programme for the countries of Africa, which paves the way for constructive action to meet their needs for organization of education and training of qualified personnel,

Emphasizing the importance of recognizing the need for further sources of financial assistance of both a capital and a recurrent nature,

I

Decides, in a spirit of solidarity, to launch an appeal to Member States, Associate Members and voluntary bodies in those States to assist through UNESCO the development of education in the countries of Africa, for the following requirements:

(a) construction of educational buildings;

(b) production of teaching aids both traditional and new;

(c) provision of overseas teachers and professors for secondary, technical and higher educational establishments;

(d) assessment of educational needs;

II

Authorizes the establishment of an emergency programme of financial aid to Member States and Associate Members in Africa, for a period of three years, 1961-1963, and to this end:

Request the Executive Board to assist the Director-General in implementing this programme, taking into consideration the conclusions of the Conference of African States to be held in 1961 and the other sources of assistance, under the following conditions:

1. *Purposes*: Capital and financial aid to meet the following four requirements:

(a) construction of educational buildings;

(b) production of teaching aids both traditional and new;

(c) provision of overseas teachers and professors for secondary, technical and higher educational establishments;

(d) assessment of educational needs.

2. *Contributions*: The programme shall receive voluntary contributions in monies without limitation as to use in a specific recipient country. These contributions shall be in easily usable currencies and they shall be the object of distinct accounting in accordance with the provisions of Article 6.6 and article 11.3 of the Financial Regulations. Their receipt and utilization shall be reported separately in the annual Financial Report of the Director-General.

3. *Participants*: All member States and Associate Members, including voluntary bodies in those States, are invited to contribute to this programme. All Member States and Associate Members in Africa may be beneficiaries of the programme. Aid shall be granted at the request and subject to the approval of the Member State or Associate Member concerned.

4. *Administration*:

(a) The Director-General shall present to the Executive Board

(i) a statement on contributions received, for information;

(ii) each project of aid, for approval;

(b) Subject to the approval of the Executive Board, the Director-General shall incur limited costs, within the framework of the approved budget, for the administration of this programme to meet the additional work of the Secretariat units concerned.

5. *Clearing House Functions*: The Director-General is authorized to publicize the financial and investment needs of the countries of Africa for the development of education, with a view to promoting multilateral, regional and bilateral cooperation among Member States. Any specific offer to meet through UNESCO an urgent and expressed need in Africa will be considered by the Executive Board;

Requests the Director-General to inform Member States periodically of the progress of these activities.

2. EDUCATION FOR INTERNATIONAL UNDERSTANDING

At the 11th Session of the General Conference of UNESCO a draft resolution (11 C/DR 114) on this subject was put before the Programme Commission by Czechoslovakia. Amendments to the resolution were submitted by the United Kingdom and by Argentina. After discussion, the delegates of Czechoslovakia and of the United Kingdom withdrew their proposals in favour of Argentina's draft resolution which, with one minor change by Belgium, was adopted unanimously by the Programme Commission. The resolution was later adopted without amendment by the General Conference.

TEXT OF RESOLUTION 1.531

The General Conference,

Recalling that, as stated in its Constitution, UNESCO was created "for the purpose of advancing, through the educational and scientific and cultural relations of the peoples of the world, the objectives of international peace and of the common welfare of mankind for which the United Nations Organization was established and which its Charter proclaims,"

Considering that every display of racial intolerance or alleged national superiority militates against these fundamental objectives and constitutes a threat to international peace, security and understanding,

Being of the opinion that a suitable upbringing, imbued with a spirit of tolerance and objectivity, can effectively help to eradicate those factors which oppose the establishment of genuine and lasting international understanding,

Condemns any display of intolerance among the different races or peoples as a violation of the high principles which prompted the creation of the United Nations and of UNESCO;

Urges Member States to redouble their efforts to ensure that education shall always be based on the principle of tolerance, the spirit of strict objectivity and the desire to maintain peaceful relations among the different nations and races;

Invites the Director-General to consider the most effective means of contributing in future, in the field of education, towards ensuring and developing international understanding, and to report on this subject to the General Conference at its twelfth session.

3. PUBLIC INFORMATION AND THE PROMOTION OF INTERNATIONAL UNDERSTANDING

The subject of the use of information media to further the cause of peace has often been debated at UNESCO's General Conference. One of the resolutions — Resolution 5.201 — in the Proposed Programme and Budget Presented to the 11th Session was the following:

"The General Conference,

"*Realizing* the important contribution that can be made by mass communication media towards the establishment of relationships of trust and peaceful co-operation between the nations and towards bringing the public to understand and support the aims and activities of UNESCO, of the United Nations and the Specialized Agencies,

"*Realizing* in particular, the opportunities offered by mass communication media for promoting in Member States a climate of opinion favourable to the fulfillment of the aims defined in the resolution on general and complete disarmament adopted by the General Assembly of the United Nations on 20 November 1959,

"1. *Invites* Member States to encourage the use of mass communication media for the purposes of education, science and culture and in the service of human welfare, international understanding and peace;

"2. *Invites* the Director-General to select, according to their contribution to the realization of these aims, those activities in UNESCO's programme which should be given priority attention by the Secretariat's information services."

When considering this resolution, the Programme Commission also had before it a draft resolution (11 C/DR/168) submitted by Burma, Ceylon and the Ukrainian Soviet Socialist Republic.

The President of the Commission pointed out that this draft resolution (see text below) concerning war propaganda could only be considered if a paragraph asking UNESCO to prepare a draft international convention outlawing the use of information media for such propaganda were omitted from the text.

Such a request would have budgetary implications and there is a time-limit set on the submission of any proposals to the General Conference.

The delegate from Ceylon then spoke, emphasizing that the intention of the draft resolution was to make a plea in the spirit of UNESCO for the utilization of information media for the strengthening of international harmony and peace and as a means of counteracting propaganda conducive to enmity and hatred among nations. It was sad, he said, to see the very tensions which UNESCO sought to remove being aggravated by propaganda. He concluded his support for the draft amendment by stating that there was a type of disarmament which concerned UNESCO — the disarmament of human minds and their liberation from fear and suspicion.

The Burmese delegate then assured the Commission that the draft resolution did not represent an attempt to introduce politics into UNESCO, but in fact only a restatement of the objectives proclaimed in UNESCO's Constitution. It was of vital importance, he said, to take active steps to restore confidence, which was a prerequisite for a true and lasting peace, founded upon the intellectual and moral solidarity of mankind.

A debate then ensued as to whether the draft resolution should replace the proposed resolution 5.201, as both contained similar ideas according to some of the delegates. The Commission decided to consider the draft resolution separately and it was adopted by a vote of 41 for, none against, with 8 abstentions.

The President then put resolution 5.201 to the vote and it was adopted unanimously. Both resolutions were later adopted with no change at a plenary session of the General Conference.

The text of resolution 5.202 (11 C/DR/168) was:

"The General Conference:

"*Understanding* the profound aspiration of all peoples to live constantly in peace and security,

"*Noting* that the main purpose of UNESCO is to contribute to international co-operation and mutual understanding,

"*Concerned* to find that in spite of the unanimous condemnation as far back as 1947 of war propaganda by all Member States of the United Nations, instances of such propaganda still exist,

"*Realizing* that war propaganda, enmity and hatred between

peoples hinder the establishment of an atmosphere of confidence between States and tends to heighten suspicion in relations between them, thereby increasing the danger of war,

"*Considering* that one of the main tasks of UNESCO is to create a public opinion favourable to the achievement of the purposes of the United Nations resolutions on the condemnation of war propaganda (1947) and on general and complete disarmament (1959) as well as of the resolution adopted at its 55th session by the Executive Board on the contribution by UNESCO to the action taken by the United Nations in favour of general and complete disarmament and of the resolution on the "Contribution by UNESCO to international understanding and peaceful co-operation," adopted by the Board at its 56th session,

"*Noting* that press and information agencies are largely responsible for the dissemination of information and can play a major role in establishing relations of confidence, mutual understanding and peaceful co-operation between States with different social and economic systems, thereby contributing effectively to the strengthening of peace,

"1. *Strongly condemns,* in accordance with Resolution 110 (II) of the United Nations General Assembly, propaganda under any form aimed at war, enmity and hatred between peoples, and considers such propaganda to be a crime against humanity.

"2. *Calls upon* all Member States:

(a) To direct their efforts to the complete realization of the recommendations contained in the resolution of the General Assembly of 3 November 1947 "on the measures which should be taken against propaganda and inciters of a new war;"

(b) to encourage and support, in every way possible, utilization of the means of information as a contribution to better mutual understanding between peoples, and thus to counteract any attempts to use press, radio, television, cinema and other means of information for propaganda which deliberately or insidiously incites violation of peace or acts of aggresion.

"3. *Requests* the Director-General to invite Member States to submit to a forthcoming session of the Executive Board, information on the measures taken in their countries for the utilization of information media for the purpose of strengthening peace, and of counteracting propaganda aimed at aggresion and war, enmity and hatred between peoples.

"4. *Entrusts* the Director-General to take the necessary measures to ensure that the activities of UNESCO in the field of information, including the issue of special radio and television programmes, posters, films, organization of exhibitions and all available means of public relations, are directed towards peace, international co-operation and understanding, thus counteracting ideas leading to war, enmity and hatred between peoples."

4. INTERNATIONAL CAMPAIGN FOR THE SAFEGUARDING OF THE MONUMENTS OF NUBIA

In reply to their requests, the Executive Board, at its 55th session (November-December 1959) decided to authorize the Director-General to assist the Governments of the United Arab Republic and the Sudan to safeguard the sites and monuments of Nubia in danger of being submerged as a result of the building of the Aswan High Dam, which the Government of the United Arab Republic has undertaken to construct with a view to the economic development of the country and the prosperity of its inhabitants.

The objectives to be achieved are as follows:

(a) *United Arab Republic*: Protection of the architectural groups of Abu Simbel and Philae, in their original settings; transfer of some 20 temples and chapels; excavation of pre-historic and archaeological sites; and assistance to the work undertaken by the Documentation and Study Centre for the History of the Art and Civilization of Ancient Egypt, in Cairo, for collecting full documentation concerning the threatened monuments.

(b) *Sudan*: Transfer of four temples; excavation of sites; and collection of documentation on the threatened monuments.

The Governments of the United Arab Republic and the Sudan have themselves organized archaeological excavations in the regions threatened with submersion, but the cost of the work is beyond their means. On 8 March 1960 therefore, the Director-General on behalf of UNESCO, launched an appeal for international cooperation and initiated a world campaign to raise contributions in cash and in the form of services and equipment. With the help of a Committee of Patrons and an International Action Committee set up by him, and with help of national committees formed for this purpose in Member States.

In return for the aid received, the Government of the United Arab Republic is prepared to cede to parties carrying out excavations half the proceeds of their finds, to authorize excavations outside the threatened area and to cede, with a view to their transfer abroad, certain temples and various objects from the State reserves. The Government of the Sudan, in accordance with the legislation in that country, cedes 50% of their finds to all parties carrying out excavations.

At the 11th session of the General Conference a working party was set up to review progress of the campaign, its aims and organization and methods of financing it.

After a lengthy exchange of views, the members of the Working Party expressed their unanimous conviction that UNESCO's basic responsibilities covered the saving, by large-scale international co-operation, of monuments which were accounted some of the most wonderful in mankind's common heritage. While it was UNESCO's duty to do all it could to enable the less well-situated nations to benefit from schooling and education, it was a matter of no less importance for the Organization to ensure that schooling and education continued to enshrine the most precious cultural values inherited from the past of the various peoples and embodied in the monuments bearing the stamp of their history and their creative genius.

Among other items, the Working Party also considered two engineering projects to save the temples of Abu Simbel. A detailed report, including two draft resolutions was submitted to the Programme Commission for approval.

The Working Party's report was adopted unanimously by the Programme Commission and the resolutions it contained were subsequently adopted without change by the General Conference:

RESOLUTION 4.413/1

The General Conference,
Having considered the information contained in the Director-General's report on the International Campaign to Save the Monuments of Nubia, including the appeal for international

co-operation in this cause launched by the Director-General, with the authorization of the Executive Board, on 8 March 1960;

Approves the steps taken by the Director-General and the Executive Board to organize the International Campaign; and

Authorizes the Director-General:

(a) to continue, in co-operation with the Governments of the United Arab Republic and the Sudan, the appropriate authorities in Member States and, in particular, national committees set up for this purpose, and the international non-governmental organizations concerned, the international campaign inaugurated on 8 March 1960;

(b) to enlist the collaboration of the International Action Committee set up to assist the Director-General in the development of this campaign;

(c) to set up, in consultation with the International Action Committee, an Executive Committee to advise and comment on the allocation and employment of the moneys collected and on the co-ordination and execution of the work;

(d) to continue to receive offers of participation from governments, public or private institutions and individuals, and to transmit these offers to the Governments of the United Arab Republic or the Sudan, according to the intention specified;

(e) to maintain and administer, in accordance with the decisions of the Executive Board, a trust fund for financial contributions;

(f) to continue to give financial assistance for the work of the Consultative Committee of Experts set up by the Government of the United Arab Republic and the group of experts set up by the Government of the Sudan; and

(g) to maintain, with the funds collected through the international campaign and with the authorization of the Executive Board, the staff and services required to ensure the success of the international campaign.

RESOLUTION 4.413/2

The General Conference,

Considering that the building of the Aswan High Dam, an imposing work undertaken by the United Arab Republic to

ensure the economic development of the country and to
increase the well-being of a hard-working population whose
numbers are growing, is also likely to entail the disappear-
ance, in the Province of Egypt and in the Sudan, of a number
of monuments and sites which are among the noblest me-
morials of the history of mankind;

Considering the requests addressed to the Director-General in
1959 by the Governments of the United Arab Republic and
of the Sudan, with a view to obtaining, through UNESCO,
international assistance for the safeguarding of these monuments and sites;

Is satisfied with the efforts made for this purpose as a result of
the steps taken by UNESCO in collaboration with the Governments of the United Arab Republic and the Sudan;

Recognizing the importance of contributions calculated to develop archeological excavations and surveys;

Noting with satisfaction that, in response to the Director-General's appeal, institutions in many countries have already
provided appreciable assistance for the execution of the
scientific work required for this purpose;

Reaffirms the extreme urgency of the action undertaken to
ensure that the relics of the past of Nubia, which form an
essential part of the cultural heritage of mankind as a whole,
survive to be admired and cherished by future generations;

Invites Member States to intensify their efforts to encourage
their institutions, both public and private, as well as any individuals likely to be interested, to take an active part in this
work of international co-operation; and

Recommends that the Governments of Member States take all
appropriate steps to ensure their own participation in this
international action, in particular by means of financial contributions towards the execution of the work most necessary
for the protection of the threatened monuments, by offers of
equipment, material or technical and scientific staff, or by
any other means which may prove effective.

Sources of Information About UNESCO

Basic documentation about UNESCO — official records, publications, general information materials, etc — is available from
various sources. In general, requests for information may be ad-

dressed to: Public Liaison Division, UNESCO, 9, Place Fontenoy, Paris 7e, France; or UNESCO's New York Office at the United Nations Building, New York 17, N. Y. United States of America. All official records and publications of the Organization may also be consulted in UNESCO depository libraries. A list of these libraries is printed in the UNESCO Information Manual No. 1: "What Is UNESCO?" — a basic document on the Organization's history, structure and programme, which is available on request from the offices above.

In addition, UNESCO National Commissions can supply information and documentation, especially concerning UNESCO affairs in a particular country. Finally, information about UNESCO is also available from United Nations Information Centres and further material may be obtained from many of the sources listed in Chapter IV.

SPECIMEN LETTER OF INVITATION

College Hall, Room 310
XYZ University
30 February 19............................

Dear ....:

XYZ University is planning to conduct a Model Security Council, to be held on 5 and 6 May, 19...................... We cordially invite the participation of a delegation from your school.

Each school may send 2 delegates and a faculty advisor. The cost per person will come to approximately .... (This is an early estimate, subject to slight revision). If your school can send a delegation to this session, please fill out the attached form and return it to us by 15 March. It is important to receive this information as soon as possible in order to notify you of your country assignment.

Each school delegation is asked to submit a brief written statement (not more than 200 words) to "show cause" why the country selected as your first choice should be assigned to your delegation. The countries most in demand will go to the school that puts up the best case. The decision of the General Committee on the matter of country assignments will be final.

The agenda topic is as follows: The question of race conflict in South Africa resulting from the policies of apartheid of the Government of South Africa.

We hope very much that you will participate in this model session and we look forward to your early reply.

Yours sincerely,
Name

....
Chairman, General Committee
Model Security Council

....
....
....

....
Name of School .... Will attend
Will not attend
Person to whom further communication should be addressed:
....

....
Country you wish to represent: (with supporting statement of not more than 200 words for your first choice only)

Permanent Members: China, France, USSR, United Kingdom, United States.
Non-Permanent Members: Ceylon, Chile, Ecuador, Liberia, Turkey, United Arab Republic. (As of 1961).
We plan to send .... delegates and a faculty advisor ....
                                No.

APPENDIX II

ANNOTATED SPECIMEN AGENDA ITEMS

(These items formed part of the agenda of the United Nations General Assembly, 15th Session, 1960)

1. SUSPENSION OF NUCLEAR AND THERMO-NUCLEAR TESTS (item proposed by India)

In requesting inclusion of this item in the agenda (Document A/4414), India noted that the General Assembly had considered the problem at its last five sessions. Last year, the Assembly had taken note of the negotiations in progress on this subject at Geneva and had expressed hope for an early agreement. It had also appealed to the states taking part in the Geneva talks to continue their present voluntary suspension of tests and had appealed to other states to desist from such tests.

However, the Indian memorandum went on, progress in the Geneva talks seemed to be less rapid than had been hoped for, and meanwhile the situation was growing worse. The growth of nuclear stockpiles, the development of new weapons, the progress made in the production of missiles and in launching satellites into outer space added to possible future tests "an additional dimension of danger." Moreover, the memorandum observed, the number of countries possessing nuclear weapons had increased and tests had taken place, in spite of the General Assembly's appeal. There was every possiblility that still more countries might be in a position to manufacture and test weapons.

In these circumstances, India considered it urgent that an agreement be reached on cessation of tests, to which all countries would adhere. India's view was that a renewed appeal should be addressed to the powers taking part in the Geneva talks to "redouble" their efforts to reach agreement, and that the Assembly should call upon all states to desist from the testing of nuclear weapons.

2. Proposal for distribution of food surpluses through the
   United Nations system

A proposal that food surpluses be distributed to the needy
peoples of the world through the United Nations was made in
the General Assembly's Second (Economic and Financial) Committee on 18 October 1960 by the United States together with
Canada, Haiti, Liberia, Pakistan and Venezuela.

The six-power draft resolution urged all members of the United
Nations and of the specialized agencies to support the world
Freedom-from-Hunger campaign launched in July 1960 by the
Food and Agriculture Organization (FAO), and suggested two
lines of action: (1) procedures should be established "without
delay" to make available, on special conditions, the "largest practicable" quantities of surplus food with the assistance of "the
United Nations system," in particular FAO; (2) a study should
be undertaken of possible additional arrangements to mobilize
foodstuffs for distribution in areas of greatest need.

The question of establishing a world food reserve to use the
surpluses of some areas to combat hunger and famine in others
came up for discussion by the General Assembly in 1954. It was
decided to ask FAO to prepare a report on the feasibility of setting up a world food reserve to help relieve emergency situations,
counteract excessive price fluctuations, and promote a rational
disposal of agricultural surpluses.

The FAO report, *Functions of a World Food Reserve — Scope
and Limitations,* was published in 1956 and discussed by the
Economic and Social Council; later, in January/February 1957,
it was discussed by the General Assembly. A further report was
requested and prepared by FAO, *National Food Reserve Policies
in Underdeveloped Countries,* and received by the Council in
1958. The Council agreed with the conclusion of the report that
food surpluses could be used to build up national food reserves,
taking into account the need for conforming with the internation-
ally-agreed principles of FAO for surplus disposal.

3. Information from Non-Self-Governing Territories

Under Article 73e of the United Nations Charter, member
states administering non-self-governing territories, other than
trust territories, transmit annually to the Secretary-General information relating to economic, social and educational conditions
in the territories they administer. Summaries and analyses of the
information given are then prepared by the Secretary-General
and are examined each year by the Committee on Information
from Non-Self-Governing Territories which reports to the Assembly.

The Committee's 1960 report to the Assembly (Document
A/4371) is primarily concerned with economic conditions. It
deals with aspects of particular interest to the Committee: trade

and banking, the shift toward a monetary economy, and other changes in the economy that might affect the living conditions of the indigenous population.

APPENDIX III

SPECIMEN RESOLUTIONS
UNITED NATIONS GENERAL ASSEMBLY
FIFTEENTH REGULAR SESSION

1. SUBJECT OF RESOLUTION: *Suspension of Nuclear and Thermo-Nuclear Tests*

DATE APPROVED: 20 December 1960

VOTE: *Part A*: 89 in favor, none against, 4 abstentions
      Part B: 83 in favor, none against, 11 abstentions

DOCUMENT NUMBERS:

COMMITTEE REPORT TO ASSEMBLY:
First Committee Report A/4680

RESOLUTION AS ADOPTED BY ASSEMBLY:
Part B: A/RES/1578 (XV)
Part A: A/RES/1577 (XV)

TEXT OF RESOLUTION

A

The General Assembly,

Recalling its resolution 1252 B (XIII) of 4 November 1958 and 1402 (XIV) of 21 November 1959.

Considering the importance and urgency of an agreement on the prohibition of nuclear and thermo-nuclear weapons tests, with effective international control,

Noting with satisfaction that further progress with regard to such an agreement has been achieved at the negotiations in Geneva since the fourteenth session of the General Assembly and that the States concerned have voluntarily suspended such tests since the autumn of 1958,

1. *Urges* the States concerned to seek a solution for the few remaining questions, so that the conclusion of the agreement will be achieved at an early date;

2. *Urges* the States concerned in these negotiations to continue their present voluntary suspension of the testing of nuclear weapons;

3. *Requests* the parties concerned to report to the Disarmament Commission and to the General Assembly the results of their negotiations.

B

The General Assembly,

Recalling its resolutions 1379 (XIV) of 20 November 1959 and 1402 (XIV) of 21 November 1959,

Continuing to bear in mind the profound concern evinced by the peoples of all countries regarding the testing of nuclear and thermo-nuclear weapons and the consequences thereof,

Recognizing that, as a result of the endeavours at Geneva of the parties concerned, substantial progress had been made towards reaching agreement on the cessation of the testing of nuclear and thermo-nuclear weapons under appropriate international control,

Recognizing further that agreement on the cessation of tests of nuclear and thermo-nuclear weapons is not only imperative but urgent,

1. *Urges* the States concerned to make every effort to reach agreement as soon as possible on the cessation of tests of nuclear and thermo-nuclear weapons under appropriate international control;

2. *Urges* the States concerned in the Geneva negotiations to continue their present voluntary suspension of the testing of nuclear and thermo-nuclear weapons, and requests other States to refrain from undertaking such tests;

3. *Requests* the States concerned in the Geneva negotiations:

(a) To keep the Disarmament Commission periodically informed of the progress of their negotiations;

(b) To report the results of their negotiations to the Disarmament Commission and the General Assembly.

2. SUBJECT OF RESOLUTION: *Provision of food surpluses to food-deficient peoples through the United Nations system*

DATE ADOPTED: 27 October 1960

VOTE: Unanimous

DOCUMENT NUMBERS:

REPORT TO ASSEMBLY: *Second Committee Report A/4551*

RESOLUTION AS ADOPTED BY ASSEMBLY:

A/RES/1496 (XV)

TEXT OF RESOLUTION

The General Assembly,

Considering that the peoples in many of the less developed countries suffer from serious shortages of food,

Noting with approval that the Food and Agriculture Organisation of the United Nations in co-operation with the United Nations, appropriate specialized agencies, Governments of Member States and non-governmental organisations, has launched a Freedom from Hunger Campaign designed as a concerted attack on the problem of providing adequate food for food-deficient peoples,

Recalling General Assembly resolutions 827 (IX) of 14 December 1954 and 1025 (XI) of 20 February 1957 and Economic and Social Council resolutions 621 (XXII) of 6 August 1956 and 685 (XXVI) of 18 July 1958 concerning international co-operation in the establishment of national food reserves,

Bearing in mind the existing opportunities for consultation and exchange of information provided by the Food and Agriculture Organisation through its Consultative Sub-Committee on Surplus Disposal,

Recognizing that the Principles of Surplus Disposal[1] and Guiding Lines[2] of the Food and Agriculture Organisation are a valuable instrument for guidance to Governments in transactions, programmes, policies, and consultations relating to the disposal and utilization of agricultural surpluses,

Recognizing further that the ultimate solution to the problem of hunger lies in an effective acceleration of economic development allowing the under-developed countries to increase their food production and enabling them to purchase more food through normal channels of international trade,

Convinced of the impelling need to solve the problem of hunger and malnutrition among many peoples and of the role which the United Nations system can play in actions designed to help solve this critical problem,

Further convinced that assistance to food-deficient peoples will help raise productivity and thus contribute to the improvement of their standard of living,

1. *Endorses* the Freedom from Hunger Campaign launched by the Food and Agriculture Organisation of the United Nations and urges all States Members of the United Nations and members of the specialized agencies to support this campaign in every appropriate way;

---

1. Food and Agriculture Organisation of the United Nations, Commodity Policy Studies, No. 10, *Functions of a World Food Reserve — Scope and Limitations* (Rome, 1956) , appendix III.
2. Ibid., para. 300

2. *Appeals* to States Members of the United Nations and members of the specialized agencies to take suitable measures to relieve the suffering of food-deficient people in other nations and assist them in their economic development and in their efforts towards a better life;

3. *Expresses the belief* that international assistance in the establishment of national food reserves in food-deficient countries is one effective transitional means of assisting accelerated economic development in the less developed countries;

4. *Invites* the Food and Agriculture Organisation, after consulting Governments of member states, the Secretary-General and appropriate specialized agencies, to establish without delay procedures — in particular for consultation and the dissemination of information — by which, with the assistance of the United Nations system, the largest practicable quantities of surplus food may be made available on mutually agreeable terms as a transitional measure against hunger, such procedures to be compatible with desirable agricultural development as a contribution to economic development in the less developed countries and without prejudice to bilateral arrangements for this purpose and compatible with the principles of the Food and Agriculture Organisation;

5. *Further invites* the Food and Agricultural Organisation, in consultation with Governments of Member States, the Secretary-General, appropriate specialized agencies and other international bodies (such as the International Wheat Council, the Wheat Utilization Committee, etc.) , to undertake a study of the feasibility and acceptability of additional arrangements, including multilateral arrangements under the auspices of the Food and Agriculture Organisation, having as their objective the mobilization of available surplus foodstuffs and their distribution in areas of greatest need, particularly in the economically less developed countries;

6. *Requests* the Director-General of the Food and Agriculture Organisation to report on action taken to the Economic and Social Council at its thirty-second session;

7. *Requests* the Secretary-General, in consultation with the Director-General of the Food and Agriculture Organisation and after such other consultations as he may deem necessary, to report to the Economic and Social Council at its thirty-second session on the role which the United Nations and the appropriate specialized agencies could play in order to facilitate the best possible use of food surpluses for the economic development of the less developed countries;

8. *Recommends* that the Secretary-General, in preparing, in consultation with the Director-General of the Food and Agriculture Organisation, the provisional programme for the joint session of the Commission on International Commodity

Trade and the Committee on Comodity Problems of the Food and Agriculture Organisation which will examine a report on the prospects of the production of, and demand for, primary commodities, include the question of the production of, and demand for, food in relation to the problem of hunger;

9. *Stresses* that any action taken or contemplated under the present resolution proceed in accordance with the Principles of Surplus Disposal and Guiding Lines of the Food and Agriculture Organisation, and, specifically, with adequate safeguards and appropriate measures against the dumping of agricultural surpluses on the international markets and against adverse effects upon the economic and financial position of those countries which depend for their foreign exchange earnings primarily on the export of food commodities, and in the recognition that the avoidance of damage to normal trading in foodstuffs will best be assured by the multilateral trading practices.

3. SUBJECT OF RESOLUTION: *Report on Economic Conditions in Non-Self-Governing Territories*

DATE APPROVED: 15 December 1960
VOTE: 75 in favor, none against, 11 abstentions
DOCUMENT NUMBERS:
COMMITTEE REPORT TO ASSEMBLY:
Fourth Committee Report A/4650
RESOLUTION AS ADOPTED BY ASSEMBLY: A/RES/1534

TEXT OF RESOLUTION

The General Assembly,

Recalling that by resolution 564 (VI) of 18 January 1952 it approved the special report drawn up in 1951 as a brief but considered indication of economic conditions in Non-Self-Governing Territories and the problems of economic development,

Recalling further that by resolution 846 (IX) of 22 November 1954 it approved another special report on economic conditions as a supplement to the 1951 report.

Recalling also that by resolution 1152 (XII) of 26 November 1957 it approved a further special report on economic conditions,

Having received and considered a further report on economic condition in Non-Self-Governing Territories prepared by the Committee on Information from Non-Self-Governing Territories at its eleventh session in 1960,

1. *Takes note* of the report on economic conditions in Non-Self-Governing Territories prepared by the Committee on Information from Non-Self-Governing Territories at its last ses-

sion and considers that this report should be studies in connexion with the other reports mentioned above;

2. *Invites* the Secretary-General to communicate this report
to Members of the United Nations responsible for the administration of Non-Self-Governing Territories, to the Economic
and Social Council, to the regional economic commissions, to
the Trusteeship Council and to the specialized agencies concerned for their consideration;

3. *Expresses its confidence* that the Members responsible for
the administration of Non-Self-Governing Territories will
bring the report to the attention of the authorities responsible
for economic development in those Territories.

APPENDIX IV

MODIFIED RULES OF PROCEDURE
FOR A MODEL GENERAL ASSEMBLY

The rules of procedure given below have been worked out by
the Collegiate Council for the United Nations (USA) and have
been widely used in model sessions held in the United States and
Canada. They have been adapted from the official *Rules of Procedure of the General Assembly* actually used at the United Nations. They have been simplified in order that the full attention
of the meeting can be directed toward the substance of the debate.
It is important not to waste time in debating procedural questions. With this guiding principle in mind, organizers of a model
meeting should feel free to revise the rules here given as they may
deem necessary.

It should be noted that each of the main organs of the United
Nations and its related agencies has its own official rules of procedure. These are issued in the working languages of the body
concerned (usually, in English, French and Spanish). Copies can
be obtained from sales agents of the body concerned. Adaptations
can be made as needed.

A copy of these rules of procedure, together with any modifica-
tion, that will be used at the model session, should be sent to each
participant well in advance of the meeting to allow time for careful study.

Agenda

RULE 1

The agenda of the General Assembly shall be drawn up by the

Organizing Committee and shall be regarded as adopted at the beginning of the session. There shall be no revisions or additions to the agenda.

RULE 2

The Organizing Committee shall allocate agenda items to the main committees of the General Assembly.

Delegations
RULE 3

The credentials of all members of delegations, having been submitted to the Secretary-General and Organizing Committee in advance of the session of the model General Assembly, shall be considered to have been approved.

The President
RULE 4

The President of the Session shall be chosen in advance of the session by the Organizing Committee.

RULE 5

The President shall:
- a) declare the opening and closing of each plenary meeting
- b) direct the discussion in plenary meetings
- c) ensure the observance of these rules
- d) accord the right to speak
- e) put questions to a vote and announce decisions
- f) rule on points of order
- g) limit the time to be allowed to speakers
- h) close the list of speakers
- i) close or adjourn debate

RULE 6

The President may not vote.

The Secretariat
RULE 7

The Secretary-General shall be appointed by the Organizing Committee in advance of each session.

RULE 8

The Secretary-General and his staff shall act in the capacity of Secretariat for all meetings of the General Assembly, and shall be responsible for advance notice of sessions, reports of committees and all documentation.

Languages

RULE 9

The model session shall be conducted in the language or languages most commonly understood in the place where the session is held. No interpretation will be provided by the organizers of the model session. However, any participant wishing to address the session in another language may do so, provided he brings his own interpreter.

Quorum

RULE 10

A majority of the Members of the General Assembly shall constitute a quorum in both Plenary meetings and Committee meetings.

Speakers

RULE 11

No representative may address the Plenary sessions or the committee meetings without having first obtained the permission of the President or the committee chairman. Speakers are called upon in order in which they signify their desire to speak. Speakers signify their desire to speak by placing their names on the speaker's list, or, in general debate, by raising their hand. A speaker may not speak if his remarks are not pertinent to the subject under discussion.

RULE 12

The President in the plenary sessions and the committee chairman in the committee meetings may limit the time to be allowed to speakers. Speakers must limit their remarks to the time allotted and will be called out of order if they speak beyond the time allotted.

Time limit on speeches

RULE 13

The President or Committee Chairman will announce the opening of the list of speakers. They may also, with the consent of the General Assembly, declare the list closed. They may, however, re-open the list if time permits.

Proposals and Amendments

RULE 14

Proposals, resolutions and amendments may be introduced orally, but a written copy must be given to the Secretary-General

who shall circulate copies to the delegations. The President and
Committee Chairman may set deadlines for the submission of
resolutions or amendments on any items.

Withdrawal of motions

RULE 15

A motion may be withdrawn by its proposer at any time before
voting on it has commenced. A motion which has been withdrawn
may be reintroduced by any member.

Reconsideration of proposals

RULE 16

When a proposal has been adopted or rejected, it may not be
reconsidered unless the General Assembly by a two-thirds majority of members present and voting so decides. Permission to speak
on a motion to reconsider shall be accorded only to two members
opposing the motion, after which it shall immediately be put to
a vote.

Adjournment and closure of debate

RULE 17

During the discussion of any matter, a representative may move
the adjournment or closure of the debate. Two representatives
may speak in favor of, two against, the motion for closure or adjournment of debate, after which the motion shall be immediately
put to the vote.

Suspension or adjournment of the meeting

RULE 18

At any time, a representative may move the suspension or adjournment of the meeting. Such a motion shall not be debated,
but shall immediately be put to a vote. The President or committee Chairman may refuse to entertain such a motion if he
feels it will prevent the meeting from completing its work.

Order of procedural motions

RULE 19

The following motions shall have precedence over all other
proposals in the following order:
   a) To suspend the meeting
   b) To adjourn the meeting
   c) To adjourn the debate
   d) To close the debate

Reports of Committees

RULE 20

Discussion of the reports of the main committees of the General Assembly shall take place in the Plenary session if the committee submitting the report shall so request.

Voting

RULE 21

Each member of the General Assembly shall have one vote.

RULE 22

In the Plenary sessions decisions on substantive questions and amendments shall be made by a majority of two thirds of the members present and voting. Abstentions are not counted as a vote. In the committee meetings decisions are made by a simple majority of those present and voting.

RULE 23

Representatives shall normally vote by show of hands or by standing. Any representative may call for a roll call vote, but no roll call votes will be taken on the following:

    a) procedural questions
    b) in the plenary, on resolutions already voted on in the main committees

Voting on a resolution in parts

RULE 24

Any representative may request that parts of a proposal or of an amendment shall be voted separately. Those parts which are approved shall then be put to the vote as a whole. If all operative parts of the proposal or of the amendment have been rejected, the proposal or the amendment shall be considered to have been rejected as a whole.

Conduct of Voting

RULE 25

After the President or committee Chairman has announced the beginning of voting, no representative shall interrupt the voting. Members may be permitted to explain their votes after the voting; the President or committee Chairman may limit the time to be allowed for such explanations.

RULE 26

When an amendment is moved to a proposal, the amendment shall be voted on first. When two or more amendments are moved to a proposal, the General Assembly shall vote first on the amendment furthest in substance removed from the original proposal, then on the amendment next furthest removed therefrom, and so on. Where, however, the adoption of one amendment necessarily implies the rejection of another amendment, the latter amendment shall not be put to the vote. A motion is considered an amendment to a proposal if it merely adds to, deletes from, or revises part of that proposal.

APPENDIX V

MODIFIED RULES OF PROCEDURE
FOR A MODEL SECURITY COUNCIL

The rules of procedure given below have been adapted from the official *Rules of Procedure of the Security Council* actually used at the United Nations. They have been modified so as to take into account the need for experienced direction of model sessions by a responsible Organizing Committee and such other practical realities as can be expected to obtain. For example, model sessions are necessarily *ad hoc* in nature, whereas, in reality, the Security Council of the United Nations is so organized as to be able to function continuously. Such further matters as the languages used at the model session should also be adjusted to suit the particular locality in which the session is held.

A copy of the rules of procedure that will be used at the model session should be sent to each participant well in advance of the meeting to allow time for careful study.

Agenda

RULE 1

The agenda of the model Security Council shall be drawn up by the Organizing Committee and sent to all participants well in advance of the meeting. The agenda shall be regarded as adopted at the beginning of the session. There shall be no revisions or additions to the agenda.

Representation and Credentials

RULE 2

Each member of the Security Council shall be represented at its meetings by an accredited representative.

Rule 3

The credentials of all representatives on the Security Council, having been submitted to the Secretary-General and the Organizing Committee in advance of the session of the model Security Council, shall be considered to have been approved.

Rule 4

Any member of the United Nations which is not a member of the Security Council may be invited, as the result of a decision of the Organizing Committee, to participate without vote, in the discussion of any question brought before the Security Council when the Organizing Committee considers that the interests of that member are especially affected. The credentials of such representatives shall be approved in the manner outlined in Rule 3.

Rule 5

Any member of the United Nations invited in accordance with the preceding rule to participate in the discussions of the Security Council may submit proposals and draft resolutions. These proposals and draft resolutions may be put to a vote only at the request of a representative on the Security Council.

The President

Rule 6

The President of the model Security Council shall be chosen in advance of the session by the Organizing Committee.

Rule 7

The President shall preside over the meetings of the Security Council and, under the authority of the Council, shall represent it in its capacity as an organ of the United Nations.

The Secretariat

Rule 8

The Secretary-General shall be appointed by the Organizing Committee in advance of the model session.

Rule 9

The Secretary-General shall act in that capacity in all meetings of the Security Council and shall be responsible for advance notice of sessions, reports of its commissions and committees and all documentation.

Rule 10

The Secretary-General may make either oral or written statements to the Security Council concerning any question under consideration by it.

Languages

RULE 11

The model session shall be conducted in the language or languages most commonly understood in the place where the session is held. No interpretation will be provided by the organizers of the model session. However, any participant wishing to address the session in another language may do so provided he brings his own interpreter.

Conduct of Business

RULE 12

A speaker's list shall be formulated under the direction of the Organizing Committee prior to each session.

RULE 13

The President shall call upon representatives in the order in which they signify their desire to speak.

RULE 14

The President may, at his discretion, impose limits of time to each speaker.

RULE 15

If a representative raises a point of order, the President shall immediately state his ruling. If it is challenged, the President shall submit his ruling to the Security Council for immediate decision and it shall stand unless overruled.

RULE 16

Proposed resolutions, amendments and substantive motions shall preferably be placed before the representatives in writing.

RULE 17

Principal motions and draft resolutions shall have precedence in the order of their submission.

Parts of a motion or of a draft resolution shall be voted on separately at the request of any representative, unless the original mover objects.

RULE 18

The following motions shall have precedence in the order named over all principal motions and draft resolutions relative to the subject before the meeting:
a) To suspend the meeting.
b) To adjourn the meeting.
c) To adjourn the meeting to a certain day or hour.

d) To refer any matter to a committee, to the Secretary-General or to a rapporteur.

e) To postpone discussion of the question to a certain day or to introduce an amendment.

Any motion for the suspension or for the simple adjournment of the meeting shall be decided without debate.

RULE 19

It shall not be necessary for any motion or draft resolution proposed by a representative on the Security Council to be seconded before being put to a vote.

RULE 20

A motion or draft resolution can at any time be withdrawn, so long as no vote has been taken with respect to it.

If the motion or draft resolution has been seconded, the representative on the Security Council who has seconded it may require that it be put to the vote as his motion or draft resolution with the same right of precedence as if the original mover had not withdrawn it.

RULE 21

If two or more amendments to a motion or draft resolution are proposed, the President shall rule on the order in which they are to be voted upon. Ordinarily, the Security Council shall first vote on the amendment furthest removed in substance from the original proposal and then on the amendment next furthest removed until all amendments have been put to the vote, but when an amendment adds to or deletes from the text of a motion or draft resolution, that amendment shall be voted on first.

RULE 22

The Security Council invite members of the Secretariat or other persons whom it considers competent for the purpose, to supply it with information or to give other assistance in examining matters within its competence.

Voting

RULE 23

Each member of the Security Council has one vote. Decisions on procedural matters are made by an affirmative vote of any seven members.

RULE 24

Decisions on other (that is, substantive) matters are made by an affirmative vote of seven members, including the concurring votes of the permanent members. (A negative vote by a permanent member on a matter of substance is popularly referred to as a "veto." In practice, an abstention by one of the permanent members is not regarded as a veto.)

RULE 25

Any member, whether permanent or non-permanent, must abstain from voting in any decision in a dispute to which it is a party.

Admission of New Members

RULE 26

Any State which desires to become a Member of the United Nations shall submit an application to the Secretary-General. This application shall contain a declaration made in a formal instrument that it accepts the obligations contained in the Charter.

RULE 27

The Secretary-General shall place the application for membership before the representatives on the Security Council.

RULE 28

The Security Council shall decide whether in its judgment the applicant is a peace-loving State and is able and willing to carry out the obligations contained in the Charter, and accordingly whether to recommend the applicant State for membership.

If the Security Council recommends the applicant State for membership, it shall forward to the General Assembly the recommendation with a complete record of the discussion.

If the Security Council does not recommend the applicant State for membership or postpones the consideration of the application, it shall submit a special report to the General Assembly with a complete record of the discussion.

APPENDIX VI

A SELECTION OF UNITED NATIONS DOCUMENTS AND PUBLICATIONS

Organizers of model sessions of the General Assembly and other United Nations bodies frequently have requested a list of selected United Nations documents and publications which would be particularly helpful for background study by participants in such sessions. The list given below has been compiled in response to these requests.

It comprises three groups of materials: (1) Pamphlets and leaflets; (2) Basic general publications; (3) the *Rules of Procedure* and the *Official Records* of the United Nations Organs, including a selection of key *Reports* presented to or drawn up by these bodies, and the *Resolutions* adopted at the session indicated.

Official Records comprise the verbatim or summary records of discussion of the General Assembly and its main committees, Security Council, Disarmament Commission, Economic and Social Council, and Trusteeship Council. These are listed by session or year for each organ. Reports and documents presented to these bodies are published as Annexes or Supplements in the Official Records. Resolutions of each of the organs are also issued as Supplements and are published in the five official languages. Language editions are indicated by the appropriate letter in parenthesis after each title: (E) English, (F) French, (E/F) English-French in one volume, (S) Spanish, (R) Russian, (C) Chinese.

Orders should include sales number, title, and language editions required. Orders may be sent to distributors for United Nations publications; to the Sales Section, United Nations, New York; the Sales Section, United Nations, Geneva, Switzerland; or to any bookseller. It should also be noted that comprehensive catalogues of United Nations publications and selected subject lists are available on request.

Prices are quoted in United States dollars, pounds sterling, and Swiss francs; however, purchases can be made in other currencies.

Pamphlets and leaflets

Basic Facts About the United Nations (E F S R C)
   60.I.7, 15 ed., 48 p., $0.25, 1/9, 1 Sw. fr.
   Also available in many other languages
Technical Assistance in Brief (E F S)
   Per hundred: $5.00, 35/6, 21.50 Sw. fr.
   Also available in many other languages

Basic general publications

Charter of the United Nations (E F S R C)
   96 p., $0.10, 9 d, 0.40 Sw. fr.
   Available also in many other languages
Everyman's United Nations (E F S)
   59.I.2 6th ed., 607 p., $3.50, 25/-, 14 Sw. fr. (English & French eds)
                            $2.50, 17/6, 10.50 Sw. fr. (Spanish ed.)
United Nations Yearbook (E)
   1959 issue 60.I.1, 660 p., $12.50, £4.10, 50 Sw. fr.
United Nations Review (E F S)
   Monthly, illus., indexed annually, Yearly subscription:
   U.S.A. and Canada: $6.00, 30/-, 24 Sw. fr; other areas $3.00, 21/-,
                                                          13 Sw. fr.

Rules of Procedure of United Nations Organs

General Assembly (E F S R C)
61.I.4, 45 p., $0.50, 3/6, 2 Sw. fr.
Security Council (E F S R)
52.I.18, 16 p., $0.25, 1/9, 1 Sw. fr.
Economic and Social Council (E F S)
58.I.3, 30 p., $0.25, 1/9, 1 Sw. fr.
Trusteeship Council (E F S)
58.I.20, 20 p., $0.15, 1/-, 0.50 Sw. fr.

Official Records: The items listed below constitute a selection of the most recent records currently available (as of December 1960) for the organ concerned. Thus, selected Reports presented to the General Assembly, 15th session, are listed although the plenary and committee records and resolutions of this session will not be issued until late in 1961. Further information concerning *Official Records* can be obtained from the Sales Section, United Nations, New York.

GENERAL ASSEMBLY OFFICIAL RECORDS, 15th SESSION

Supplements

No. 1 *Annual Report of the Secretary-General on the Work of the Organization.* 16 June 1959 — 15 June 1960. 103 p. (A/4390) $1.50, 10/6, Sw. fr.

No. 1A *Introduction to the Annual Report of the Secretary-General on the Work of the Organization.* 16 June 1959 — 15 June 1960. 8 p. (A/4390/Add. 1) $0.35, 2/6, 1.50 Sw. fr.

No. 2 *Report of the Security Council to the General Assembly.* 16 July 1958 — 15 July 1959. 43 p. (A/4494) $0.75, 5/-, 3 Sw. fr.

No. 3 *Report of the Economic and Social Council.* 1 August 1959 — 5 August 1960. 91 p. (A/4415) $1.50, 10/6, 6.50 Sw. fr.

No. 4 *Report of the Trusteeship Council.* 7 August 1959 — 30 June 1960. 170 p. (A/4404) $2.00, 14/-, 8.50 Sw. fr.

No. 5A *Budget for the Financial Year 1961.* 11 p. (A/4687) $0.35, 2/6, 1.50 Sw. fr.

No. 9 *Report of the International Law Commission,* covering the work of its twelfth session, 25 April — 1 July 1960. 38 p. (A/4425) $0.50, 3/6, 2.00 Sw. fr.

No. 11 *Report of the United Nations High Commissioner for Refugees.* May 1959 — May 1960. 35 p. (A/4378/Rev. 1) $0.50, 3/6, 2.00 Sw. fr.

No. 12 *Report of the Committee on South West Africa.* 67 p. (A/4464) $0.75, 5/-, 3.00 Sw. fr.

No. 14 *Annual Report of the Director of the United Nations Relief and Works Agency for Palestine Refugees in the Near East.* 1 July 1959 — 30 June 1960. 34 p. (A/4478) $0.50, 3/6, 2 Sw. fr.

No. 15 *Report of the Committee on Information from Non-Self-Governing.* 69 p. (A/4371) $0.75, 5/-, 3.00 Sw. fr.

No. 16 *Resolutions,* Vol. I, 20 September — 20 December 1960. 71 p. (A/4684) $1.00, 7/-, 4.00 Sw. fr.
Resolutions, Vol. II, 7 March — 21 April 1961, to be issued.

GENERAL ASSEMBLY OFFICIAL RECORDS,
14th SESSION

Issued in the five official languages: E F S R C

Plenary Meetings: Verbatim records (795th-857th), 15 September — 13 December 1959. 791 p., $9.50, 67/-, 40.50 Sw. fr.
Special Political Committee: Summary records, 15 September — 9 December 1959. 219 p., $3.00, 21/-, 13.00 Sw. fr.
First Committee (Political and Security Questions): Summary records, 15 September — 12 December 1959. 294 p., $3.50, 25/-, 15.00 Sw. fr.
Second Committee (Economic and Financial Questions): Summary records, 15 September — 4 December 1959. 357 p., $4.00, 28/6, 17.00 Sw. fr.
Third Committee (Social, Humanitarian and Cultural Questions: Summary records, 15 September — 7 December 1959, 347 p., $4.00, 28/6, 17.00 Sw. fr.
Fourth Committee (Trusteeship): Summary records, 15 September — 11 December 1959. 701 p., $8.00, 57/-, 34.50 Sw. fr.

Supplements

No. 1 - 15:   These follow the same pattern of publication for each section; see 15th session given above.
No. 16:   *Resolutions adopted by the General Assembly during its 14th session,* 15 September — 13 December 1959. 68 p., $1.00, 7/-, 4.00 Sw. fr.
Index to Proceedings of the General Assembly, 14th Session, 15 September — 13 December 1959. 117 p. (Sales No. 60.I.11), $1.50, 10/6, 6.50 Sw. fr.

SECURITY COUNCIL OFFICIAL RECORDS,
15th YEAR

Issued in the five official languages: E/F S R C

Question of race conflict in South Africa: 851st-856th meeting: 30 March — 1 April 1960. 6 fascicules: $0.35, 2/6, 1.50 Sw. fr., per fascicule, except 852nd meeting, $0.50, 3/6, 2 Sw. fr.
Discussion relating to the U-2 incident: 857th-863rd meeting: 23-27 May 1960. 7 fascicules: $0.35, 2/6, 1.50 Sw. fr., per fascicule.

ECONOMIC AND SOCIAL COUNCIL OFFICIAL
RECORDS, 30th SESSION
Issued in E F S

Summary records of meetings (1112th - 1134th), 5 July — 5 August 1960. 164 p., $2.00, 14/-, 8.50 Sw. fr.

Supplements

No. 1   *Resolutions, 30th session,* 5 July — 5 August 1960. 30 p. (E/3422) $0.50, 3/6, 2 Sw. fr.
No. 1A   *Resolutions 30th session, resumed,* 21-22 December 1960. 4 p. (E/3422/Add. 1) $0.35, 2/6, 1.50 Sw. fr.
No. 2   *Economic Commission for Asia and the Far East.* Annual report, 20 March 1959 — 21 March 1960. 77 p. (E/3340) $1.00, 7/-, 4.00 Sw. fr.

No. 3   *Economic Commission for Europe.* Annual report, 7 May 1959 — 7 May 1960. 85 p. (E/3349) $1.00, 7/-, 4.00 Sw. fr.

No. 4   *Economic Commission for Latin America.* Annual report, 24 May 1959 — 29 March 1960. 50 p. (E/3333) $0.75, 5/-, 3.00 Sw. fr.

No. 5   *Technical Assistance Committee.* Annual report of the Technical Assistance Board for 1959. 120 p. (E/3337) $1.50, 10/6, 6.50 Sw. fr.

No. 6   *Commission on International Commodity Trade.* Report of the eighth session, 2-13 May 1960. 21 p. (E/3383) $0.35, 2/6, 1.50 Sw. fr.

No. 7   *Commission on the Status of Women.* Report of the fourteenth Session, 24 March — 14 April 1960. 26 p. (E/3360) $0.35, 2/6, 1.50 Sw. fr.

No. 8   *Commission on Human Rights.* Report of the sixteenth session, 29 February — 18 March 1960. 33 p. (E/3335) $0.50, 3/6, 2.00 Sw. fr.

No. 9   *Commission on Narcotic Drugs.* Report of the fifteenth session, 25 April — 13 May 1960. 44 p. (E/3385) $0.75, 5/-, 3.00 Sw. fr.

No. 10   *Economic Commission for Africa.* Annual report, 7 January — 6 February 1960. 42 p. (E/3320) $0.50, 3/6, 2.00 Sw. fr.

No. 11   *Governing Council of the Special Fund.* Report on its third and fourth sessions, 8-10 December 1959 and 25-27 May 1960 18 p. (E/3398) $0.35, 2/6, 1.50 Sw. fr.

No. 12   *Statistical Commission.* Report of the eleventh session, 20 April — 5 May 1960. 24 p. (E/3375) $0.35, 2/6, 1.50 Sw. fr.

Annexes, 30th session: To be issued.

Index to proceedings, 30th session. 35 p. (Sales No. 61.I.5) $0.50, 3/6, 2.00 Sw. fr.

TRUSTEESHIP COUNCIL OFFICIAL RECORDS,
26th SESSION
Issued in E F

Summary records of meetings (1051st - 1134th), 14 April — 30 June 1960. 560 p. $7.00, 50/-, 30 Sw. fr.
Supplements
No. 1   *Resolutions, 26th session,* 14 April — 30 June 1960. 32 p. (T/1549) $0.50, 3/6, 2.00 Sw. fr.

No. 2   Report of United Nations Visiting Mission to Tanganyika. 59 p. (T/1550) $0.75, 5/-, 3.00 Sw. fr.

No. 3   Report of United Nations Visiting Mission to Ruanda-Urundi. 72 p. (T/1538) $1.00, 7/-, 4.00 Sw. fr.

Annexes, 26th session, 14 April — 30 June 1960. 349 p. $3.50, 25/-, 15 Sw. fr.
Index to Proceedings, 26th session, 14 April — 30 June 1960. 25 p. (Sales No. 61.I.2) . $0.50, 3/6, 2.00 Sw. fr.

APPENDIX VII

UNITED NATIONS INFORMATION CENTRES

ACCRA
United Nations Information Centre
U. N. Office Quarters near Independence Arch
Post Box 2339
Accra, Ghana
Area Covered: Gambia, Ghana, Guinea, Nigeria, Sierra Leone

ADDIS ABABA
United Nations Information Office
United Nations Economic Commission for Africa
Adua Square
P. O. Box 3001
Addis Ababa, Ethiopia
Area Covered: Ethiopia

ATHENS
United Nations Information Centre
25A Jan Smuts Street
Athens, Greece
Area Covered: Cyprus, Greece, Israel, Turkey

BANGKOK
United Nations Information Officer
Economic Commission for Asia and the Far East
Sala Santitham
Bangkok, Thailand
Area Covered: Cambodia, Laos, Thailand, Federation of Malaya and Singapore, Vietnam

BELGRADE
United Nations Information Centre
1, Trg. Marksa i Engelsa, br. 1
Post Office Box 157
Belgrade, Yugoslavia
Area Covered: Albania, Yugoslavia

BOGOTA
Centro de Information de las Naciones Unidas.
Calle 19, Numero 7-30 Septimo Piso
Post Office Box No. 65-67
Bogota, Colombia
Area Covered: Colombia, Ecuador, Venezuela

BUENOS AIRES
Centro de Informacion de las Naciones Unidas
Charcas 684, 3 F
Buenos Aires, Argentina
Area Covered: Argentina, Paraguay, Uruguay

CAIRO
United Nations Information Centre
Sharia El Shams
Imm, Tagher
Garden City
Cairo, United Arab Republic
Area Covered: Iraq, Jordan, Lebanon, Saudi Arabia, Sudan, United Arab Republic

COLOMBO
United Nations Information Centre
P. O. Box 1505
Colombo 3, Ceylon
Area Covered: Ceylon

COPENHAGEN
United Nations Information Centre
37 H. C. Andersen's Boulevard
Copenhagen, Denmark
Area Covered: Denmark, Finland, Iceland, Norway, Sweden

DAR-ES-SALAAM
United Nations Information Centre
P. O. Box 9182
Dar-Es-Salaam, Tanganyika
Area Covered: Tanganyika

DJAKARTA
United Nations Information Officer
76 Kebon Sirih
Djakarta, Indonesia
Area Covered: Indonesia

GENEVA
Information Service, European Office
Palais des Nations
Geneva, Switzerland
Area Covered: Austria, Bulgaria, Hungary, Poland, Romania, Germany, Switzerland

KABUL
United Nations Information Centre
c/o U N/TAB Resident Represent-
ative
Sher Pur
Post Office Box 5
Kabul, Afghanistan
Area Covered: Afghanistan

KARACHI
United Nations Information Centre
Strachen Road
Post Office Box No. 349, G. P. O.
Karachi 1, Pakistan
Area Covered: Pakistan

LIMA
United Nations Information Office
c/o Resident Representative of the
UN Technical Assistance Board
Ministerio de Hacienda, Piso 11
Avenida Abancay
Apartado 4480, Naciones Unidas
Lima, Peru
Area Covered: Bolivia, Peru

LONDON
United Nations Information Centre
14/15 Stratford Place
London, W. 1, England
Area Covered: Ireland, Nether-
lands, United Kingdom and Brit-
ish Dependencies except British
West African Territories of the
Bambia, Nigeria, and Sierra Le-
one

MANILA
United Nations Information Centre
Corner of Taft Avenue and Isaac
Peral
Post Office Box 2149
Manila, Philippines
Area Covered: The Philippines

MEXICO CITY
Centro de Informacion de las Na-
ciones Unidas
Hamburgo 63, 3er piso
Mexico 6, D. F., Mexico
Area Covered: Cuba Dominican
Republic, Mexico

MONROVIA
United Nations Information Office
Post Office Box 274
24 Broad Street
Monrovia, Liberia
Area Covered: Liberia

MOSCOW
United Nations Information Centre
15 Hohlovski Pereulok, Apartment
36
Moscow, U. S. S. R.
Area Covered: Byelorussian S S R,
Ukrainian S S R, U. S. S. R.

NEW DELHI
United Nations Information Centre
21 Curzon Road
New Delhi, India
Area Covered: Ceylon, India, Nepal

PARIS
Centre d'Information des Nations
Unies
26 Avenue de Ségur
Paris 7, France
Area Covered: Belgium, Republic
of France and states and territories of the Community, Luxem-
bourg

PRAGUE
United Nations Information Centre
Panska, 5
Praha II, Czechoslovakia
Area Covered: Czechoslovakia

RANGOON
United Nations Information Centre
12, Newlyn Road
Rangoon, Burma
Area Covered: Burma

RIO DE JANEIRO
United Nations Information Centre
Rua Mexico 11, Grupo 1502
Caixa Postal 1750
Rio de Janeiro, Brazil

ROME
United Nations Information Centre
Palazzetto Venezia
Piazza San Marco 51
Rome, Italy
Area Covered: Italy

SAN SALVADOR
Centro de Informacion de las Na-
ciones Unidas
Edificio de la Gran Logia Cuscatlan
8a Avenida Sur, Numero 126
Apartado Postal 1114
San Salvador, El Salvador
Area Covered: Costa Rica, El Sal-
vador, Guatemala, Honduras,
Nicaragua, Panama

SANTIAGO
Economic Commission for Latin
America
Avenida Providencia 871
Santiago, Chile
Area Covered: Chile

SYDNEY
United Nations Information Centre
44 Martin Place
Box 4030, General Post Office
Sydney, Australia
Area Covered: Australia, New Zealand

TEHERAN
United Nations Information Centre
Heshmat Dowleh
Khiaban Keyvan
Teheran, Iran
Area Covered: Iran

TOKYO
United Nations Information Centre
New Ohtemachi Building, Room
210
4, 2-chome, Ohtemachi
Chiyoda-ku
Tokyo, Japan
Area Covered: Japan

TUNIS
United Nations Information Centre
Boite Postale 863
Pavillon O N U
Place du Gouvernement
Tunis, Tunisia
Area Covered: Libya, Tunisia

USUMBURA
United Nations Information Centre
Usumbura, Ruanda-Urundi
Area Covered: Ruanda-Urundi

WASHINGTON
United Nations Information Centre
Suite 714
1028 Connecticut Avenue, N. W.
Washington 6, D. C.

APPENDIX VIII

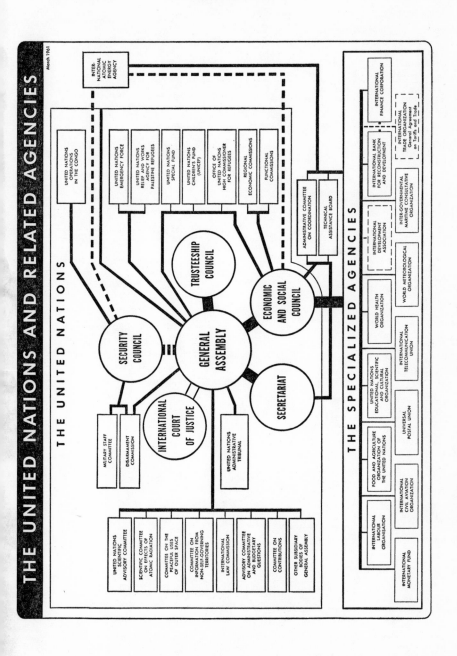

THE UNITED NATIONS AND RELATED AGENCIES